# THE PATH TO SELF-LOVE

# &

# WORLD DOMINATION

Break Free from Self-Limiting Beliefs
and Embrace Your Power

## Heidi Green, PsyD

Health Communications, Inc.
Boca Raton, Florida

*www.hcibooks.com*

Library of Congress Cataloging-in-Publication Data
is available through the Library of Congress

ISBN-13: 978-0-7573-2368-3 (Paperback)
ISBN-10: 0-7573-2368-5 (Paperback)
ISBN-13: 978-0-7573-2369-0 (ePub)
ISBN-10: 0-7573-2369-3 (ePub)

The material in this book is intended for education. It is not meant to take the place of diagnosis and treatment by a qualified medical practitioner or therapist. No expressed or implied guarantee of the effects of the use of the recommendations can be given or liability taken.

All identifying characteristics, including names, have been changed to protect the privacy of the individuals described. Moreover, each case example is largely fictional and created by using themes from therapy clients over the years.

Publisher: Health Communications, Inc.
1700 NW 2nd Avenue
Boca Raton, FL 33432-1653

*Cover design by Larissa Hise Henoch*
*Interior design and formatting by Lawna Patterson Oldfield*

# CONTENTS

*This book is dedicated with love*
*to my grandmother Mary Jane Burch, and*
*to my daughters, Alex, Katie, and Delaney.*
*May you always love yourselves*
*as fiercely as I love you.*

# ACKNOWLEDGMENTS

My heart is full of gratitude for the many friends and colleagues who contributed their wisdom to this book. To my longtime friend, Shauna Reiser, thank you for being my first editor. Your contributions to my early drafts were invaluable. Many thanks to Catherine Lowrey, my dear friend and the first psychologist to provide clinical feedback for this work. Sara Decker, thank you for providing feedback from the consumer point of view.

To Dr. Marcus Earle, my most cherished mentor, my gratitude for you extends far beyond the parameters of this book. Thank you for your wise counsel, unmitigated support, encouragement, and genuine care for me as a human. I am a better psychologist for knowing you, but more important, I am a better person.

Finally, to Camilla Michael, Allison Janse, and the team at HCI Books, thank you for taking a chance on me. Thank you for believing in my message and trusting me to deliver it. I am so grateful for all the hard work and dedication put into bringing my book to life.

# INTRODUCTION

*Whatever the question,*
*the answer is love.*

—Dr. Wayne Dyer

I suppose a book with such a lofty promise in the title requires a few qualifiers. Spoiler alert: Reading this book is unlikely to result in actual world domination. That said, I intend to set you on the path to dominate your own world, be the master of your destiny, and create the life of your dreams. This is not a lofty promise. Although it's a big undertaking, it is also a realistic possibility.

You picked up this book for a reason. Your inner critic is running rampant. Your self-limiting beliefs are controlling your life. You have big dreams but lack the self-confidence to pursue them. You feel unworthy. You long for inner peace and self-love. I get it.

Wherever you are in your life right now, however treacherous the journey seems, whatever dark cavern you may have wandered into, there is hope for you. You are powerful, capable, beautiful, and deserving. You may not feel that today, but do not fret. I am going to help you understand why you may not feel that way now and show you how you can rewire your self-limiting thoughts to reach your full potential. Reading this book will give you the tools you need to love yourself fully, trust in your capabilities, and live an abundant life. I am going to help you create your personal Self-Love Suitcase, so to speak: six traits that must be cultivated on your journey for a happier, more awesome you. These traits are self-kindness, self-acceptance, self-parenting, self-commitment, self-forgiveness, and self-respect. Through reading this book and following the exercises within, you will develop your tool kit and strengthen the self-love needed for a happier, more abundant life.

So why self-love? Why is it important? As a clinical psychologist, I have had the great honor of sitting in front of people from every walk of life. I've worked with young women, old men, cancer fighters, trauma survivors, addicts, celebrities, couples, and families. I have seen the strong side of women who were abused as children, abandoned by their fathers, or cheated on by their husbands. I have seen the tender side of men who stand accused of murder and assault. I've sat with divorcing couples as they try to figure out how to avoid damaging their children, and with older parents while they make amends to the adult children they wounded decades ago.

Each client I've worked with has been a teacher to me as much as I've been a healer for them. Their stories have become a part of my life story. They have taught me about the spirit of humanity. I have worked with people from many different walks of life whose stories and struggles are vastly different. Yet I have seen very distinct themes emerge in each one of their quests for healing.

As I bear witness to these journeys, I see how painful life experiences can strip people of their innate ability to feel and practice self-love. My work with clients has become an exercise in finding and rescuing the young person they once were so they can become the adult they were always meant to be. No matter who the person is or what their life experiences may entail, time and again that journey consistently and predictably winds itself toward the same beautiful destination: Love. It has become increasingly clear to me over the years that the secret to happiness lies, above all else, in your ability to love the most important person you will ever know: you. That's why self-love is so important. Your entire life's happiness depends on it.

Loving oneself is far more complicated than it may seem. It may appear on the surface that self-love is synonymous with self-esteem, but it isn't quite that simple. Self-love requires more than just holding yourself in high regard. It involves understanding your struggles and weaknesses through a lens of compassion. It insists you speak to yourself with kindness. Self-love mandates that you forgive yourself when you have failed or hurt others. Finally, to truly love yourself you must be humble, gentle, and meticulous in the way you treat all people, yourself included. Honoring oneself is not selfish or entitled. Sometimes honoring yourself requires setting boundaries that can upset or disappoint others. A self-loving person recognizes this will happen on occasion and knows it is okay.

On the other hand, a self-loving person will be able to honor others even when they must disappoint them. If you are genuinely honoring yourself, you will never be cruel or malicious in your intentions or delivery toward others. You will set boundaries in ways that are respectful and gracious, without holding yourself responsible for how others receive your limits.

## What Is Self-Love?

I created a simple definition of self-love for this book. Essentially, self-love is the marriage between self-esteem and self-compassion. If we were to examine self-love with a Venn diagram, we would see where the self-respect and confidence of self-esteem merge with the empathic, loving-kindness of self-compassion.

Before I became a navigator down the road of self-love, I took my own arduous journey. I was lost in a forest of self-loathing and despair. I faced down the monsters of my past and rescued the little girl I was many years ago. I learned how to love her as if she were my daughter. It wasn't until I could look her in the eyes and walk through my adult life holding on to her that I finally let go of my old wounds and became the adult I wanted to be.

Since that awakening, I have made the journey countless times with those who come to my office looking for peace of heart. The trek is different for each of us. I have come to be flexible and patient as clients learn to harness their unique set of strengths and tackle their challenges. Each time I take another traveler on the expedition toward happiness, we inevitably wind up on the path of self-love. It is on that path where they become ready to travel the roads without me as their guide. They come to a place where they realize their strength, understand the fullness of their potential, and feel prepared to guide themselves into the life they desire. This is where I intend to take you.

I wrote this book with two primary objectives in mind. My first objective is to give you a strong understanding of yourself and your struggles. I will provide you with many case examples that will present a wide range of people and their experiences. I explain how people develop their specific challenges and personal shortcomings based on their unique journeys. I will help you connect to your own story and create an understanding of how your life experiences led to your specific strengths and weaknesses. Following this path will allow you to become gentler and more compassionate toward yourself so you can develop a kinder inner voice.

My second objective is to outline the steps for using your new understanding to rewire the way you see yourself, talk to yourself, and interact with your world. Through this process, you can expect to increase your sense of self-worth, your belief in your capabilities, and your love for yourself. You will recognize the magnificent creation you are and harness your innate power. You will realize your full potential and become the master of your own life. Strap in, we're going for a ride.

# Part One:

# THE WOUNDED CHILD INSIDE YOU

# Chapter One

# Your Inner Voice

*You really have to love yourself to get*
*anything done in this world.*

—Lucille Ball

We need to discuss the way you talk to yourself. How does the voice inside your head sound? Is it kind and encouraging? Is it boastful and grandiose? Is it, perhaps, critical and demeaning? Your inner dialogue is a compilation of all the points of view you have heard throughout your life. Your parents, or the people who raised you, set the stage for the voice you will use to speak to yourself in adulthood. Other prominent figures also contribute to that voice. Siblings, teachers, coaches, and friends all add pieces to the voice that will eventually sound like your own.

If you were fortunate, the people who raised you repeatedly told you that you were valuable and important. They reinforced that your needs mattered and that your voice should be heard and honored. Children need adult caregivers who validate their ideas and feelings and who encourage them to express all emotions, not just "positive" ones. The most astute parents will not only allow their children to be angry, tired, frightened, hurt, or disappointed but will also teach their children how to soothe and regulate these emotions. Unfortunately, even the most well-meaning parents often miss this critical life lesson. Usually, it's because they never learned it themselves.

As a result, loving parents can still be impatient, critical, selfish, and unresponsive. Parents are, after all, just imperfect people trying their best to traverse an imperfect world. Every person sees the world through the lens of their personal experiences. I try not to be too hard on parents. I understand that most are trying to do right by their children, even when their approaches are ill-informed and unhelpful.

It's unlikely that a critical or controlling parent is maliciously trying to create an anxious, insecure child. More likely, they want their child to be responsible and successful, and to make good decisions. They probably don't see how their regular criticism causes their child to be unsure of themselves.

I'd like to tell you a story to give this idea more meaning. I'll provide several hypothetical case examples throughout this book. As you read them, think about how you can relate the concepts to your own life story. Your story may be completely different from the one presented, but the general ideas are applicable to us all.

✦ ✦ ✦

## Maria's Story

"Maria" was in her twenties when she decided it was time for a change. She struggled with self-esteem and negative self-talk. She was talented in athletics like her father, who coached her soccer and softball teams when she was a girl. Maria recalled how her father screamed at her on the field, embarrassing her in front of her peers. She noted that even though she was the strongest athlete on the team, her father often appeared frustrated and disappointed in her every time she failed to score or had the ball stolen by another player. She lamented that he ruined her love of sports and made her feel she was only "good enough" when she was perfect and on point.

Maria tried to get validation from her mother when she was young around her hurt feelings, but her mom always defended the actions of her father. She said things like "He just wants you to be the best," and "He is only hard on you because he loves you." Of course, Maria's parents loved her deeply. Her father's investment in her was genuine. They weren't wealthy, but Maria's parents spent considerable money on her athletic activities, and they were always present for her events. They showed her how much they loved her in many meaningful ways, but they also inadvertently sent her some very damaging messages.

Maria's father not only yelled at and embarrassed her on the field but went into agonizing, detailed lectures after practices and games about what she did wrong. He never intended to make Maria feel that she was worthy only when she was succeeding, but that is precisely what he did. Moreover, her parents sent her the message that criticism is an expression of love. The statement "He is only hard on you because he loves you" taught Maria to expect those who care about her to continually judge, condemn, and disapprove of her. Accordingly, she not only developed an internal dialogue that was harsh and demeaning but she came to expect that sort of treatment from others.

Maria's mom and dad made an all-too-common mistake of well-meaning parents. Most parents don't want to create self-doubting children who think they are lovable only when they are the best. They certainly aren't trying to teach their kids that they can't trust their own judgment or make them afraid to ever make a mistake. They aren't trying to shape their child into an adult who feels they constantly must prove their worth to others because internally they believe themselves not to be "good enough." Unfortunately, this is often the unintentional aftereffect of critical parenting.

Even cases less overt than Maria's can have lasting, damaging effects. Some parents aren't so blatantly critical, but they largely ignore their children unless the children are actively succeeding. Children in these homes learn they must perform to be seen and to get the love and validation they need. In cases like this, they are given the message that they are not innately lovable and worthy, but that love must be earned.

✦ ✦ ✦

Now I want you to think back on the messages you took in about yourself as a child. Hopefully you received plenty of positive affirmations about how smart, talented, and capable you were. It is likely, though, that you also received some unhealthy messages about yourself. These messages are often subtle and enter our identities without our conscious awareness. Identifying the underlying core beliefs we hold about ourselves is a critical first step on the path to self-love.

As an example, think for a moment about the messages you took in about your physical appearance. Did you learn you were a "pretty girl" or a "strong boy"? Maybe you were chubbier, weaker, or shorter than others. Perhaps you discovered your "big nose," "frizzy hair," or freckles made you different from other kids. Children long to be accepted, and we often seek sameness with our peers. We learn early on that different is bad, so if you were bigger, smaller, poorer, or quieter than your peers, you probably believed something was "wrong" with you.

In addition to direct, verbal messages, you probably internalized beliefs based on nonverbal messages you received in childhood. The examples here are endless. Perhaps you got dirty looks from the popular kids at school. Maybe your mom gave an exasperated sigh when you asked her to play with you, or your dad looked bored and uninterested when you showed him the A you got on your book report. Nonverbal messages can be just as profound and hurtful as verbal messages.

Childhood messages create the inner voice we take with us into adulthood. They become the foundation on which other beliefs are laid. As we move through life, we seek to confirm or reject messages we get about ourselves and our environment.

## Negativity Bias

Unfortunately, we often give more weight to the negative messages than the positive ones. Psychologists refer to this as the *negativity bias*. There is an adaptive function to this human condition. Let's say you have a hundred good or neutral experiences with a dog. Then you have one experience in which a dog unexpectedly bites you and causes significant injury. This one experience is going to supersede the many others you have had. This cognitive function serves to protect you. You need to remember the negative experience with more strength so you can protect yourself in similar circumstances in the future. Your brain wants you to put that "bad" experience in the forefront of your mind so you can keep yourself safe around other dogs you encounter in your life. It is easy to see the adaptive survival mechanism at play in the negativity bias. It keeps us alive so it's a good thing, but it also creates some challenges for us.

The biggest challenge is that our brains are not sophisticated enough to distinguish between physical danger and emotional danger. If children on the school bus call you a "loser" because your parents can't afford to buy you designer clothes, that experience is going to cause emotional pain. Your brain wants you to remember the painful message so you can develop skills to protect yourself from being called hurtful names in the future. The inner critic is born from that desire to protect yourself. Your brain thinks it can keep you safe from criticism, rejection, and pain if it is constantly pointing out all the things that might be wrong with you. It constantly sends you messages about what you need to do differently to make yourself likable and worthy. It thinks it is helping you, but this thinking is flawed.

Listening to your inner critic may make you an adult with a chip on your shoulder, always trying to prove to others that you aren't a loser because deep down you think you are. Perhaps you become an adult who finds your weaknesses intolerable. You may be perfectionistic, overly demanding, and critical. Maybe you push yourself to be the best in everything you do because anything less than perfect is a failure by your standards. Only when you have the best job, live in the best house, drive the best car, and are married to the best spouse will you convince yourself you aren't the loser kid you once were on the school bus.

The sad truth is, no amount of external proof will ever convince you that you aren't a loser because you already believe you are. You could become an unfillable pit of self-doubt and insecurity, desperately looking for the next thing to fill you up and make you feel temporarily "good enough." Unfortunately, you will just be chasing an insatiable thirst for the rest of your life if you can't learn to fill your wound with self-love.

# Find Your True Voice

You need to decipher the many voices in your head. You must filter out the voices of your past that speak in hateful tones and with unkind words. "You're never going to be successful at that. You're so stupid. I can't believe you said that. Nobody likes you. Just give up." Whose voice is that? It isn't yours. Yours is a voice of love, encouragement, and determination. Yours is a voice of kindness, assuredness, and gentle strength. It may be buried way down deep. It may have been silent for so many years, you don't remember it existing at all. That's okay. It's still in there. We're going to find it.

You may be wondering, "How do I know which voice is mine? How do you know my original inner voice was kind and loving?" All you need to do to answer these questions is spend a little time with a child whose original voice has not yet been tainted by the outside world. One of the sweetest representations of a child's pure delight in themselves is on a once-viral video titled "Jessica's Daily Affirmation." I have uploaded the video for your viewing pleasure to my website, drheidigreen.com. There you will find a video of an adorable young girl with curly blond hair talking to herself in the mirror. Sweet Jessica says to herself with enthusiasm, "I like my hair! I like my pajamas! I like my whole house! I can do anything good!" Jessica still has her original voice. Her inner voice tells her she is beautiful, strong, capable, and kind.

Another easy example is to observe a preschool classroom and ask the children about their talents. Young children will almost always tell you they are good at things with which they have little to no experience. "Who is a great artist?" Hands go flying up. "Who is a fast runner?" Hands shoot up again. Children are excited to show off their capabilities no matter what their skill level. Every "Hey Mom, watch this!" kid at the park or public swimming pool can prove that point. The human mind is designed to love and encourage itself, to believe in its capabilities and approach life with enthusiasm and wonder. It is only through painful external experiences that we lose our innate, positive mindset.

### Does a Critical Voice Motivate?

People sometimes think the critical voice in their heads is a motivating factor. When I speak of self-kindness, clients often tell me they need their harsh internal voice to motivate them, to keep them from becoming lazy or complacent. I challenge this belief right away with a hypothetical scenario.

Let's say you are tasked with teaching a young child to ride a bike. What is your approach? Likely, you will begin with a little pep talk: "Riding a bike is fun! You are so big! You can do it!" Then you will sprinkle in some understanding around the child's uncertainty and offer support: "I will be right here the whole time. I'll hold the back of the seat so you don't fall until you can do it on your own." Once the child is up and riding, you offer an enthusiastic celebration: "You're doing it! You're a great bike rider!" Then, when the inevitable first fall happens, you offer both compassion and encouragement: "Are you okay? Let me clean the scratch. You were doing so well. Sometimes falls happen. Don't worry. You can get back up and try again when you're ready. I'm proud of you!"

When we are being our best adult selves, we don't motivate children by criticizing and insulting them. We don't say to them, "Listen, kid. You're being a wimp. Riding a bike is easy. Just get up and do it!" Why don't we speak that way? Because our innate wisdom tells us the way to encourage someone to succeed is to do it through love, not insults, threats, or shame.

The response I sometimes get next is, "Well yes, that might work for a child, but I'm an adult. I'm not going to coddle myself like that." I follow up with "How do you motivate and encourage a friend?" When you are being a good friend, you offer motivation and encouragement, not unlike you would to a child. You follow a similar script, which includes sharing your belief in them and offering empathy for their doubts and fear. Then you express encouragement and enthusiasm in their favor. We don't motivate our friends with disparaging remarks about what a failure they will be if they can't get it right. We don't tell them they aren't smart enough or talented enough. We don't say to our friends, "Just give up. You don't have what it takes."

Think back for a moment to the most valuable mentors you have had in your adult life. Whether a boss, professor, coach, or even a therapist, they each had a positive impact on you because they motivated you with kindness. We value those who believe in us when we don't believe in ourselves. People who offer us guidance, support, and encouragement when we struggle to muster it up for ourselves are the ones we look back on with fondness and gratitude.

In *Animals Make Us Human*, Dr. Temple Grandin discusses how distress impedes learning in animals, just as it does in humans. All mammals innately feel rage, panic, and fear. These emotional experiences interfere with learning and brain development.

We know that pressure, criticism, and humiliation from others make us nervous and interrupt learning. But when it comes to talking to ourselves, we can get confused. We might use self-criticism to get something done, and then when we succeed (despite the criticism), we falsely associate self-criticism with effective motivation. In our hearts, we know loving inspiration is the best motivator. It's why we give it to others. It's why we value people who offer it to us. So why do we fail to give it to ourselves?

People often talk to themselves in a way they would never speak to another human being. I am guilty of this as well. I know I have been terribly unkind to myself, more so than I would be to a person I seriously dislike. There is only one explanation. That is not my voice. I know my voice. I hear it every day when I speak to people. I am not unkind. I am a good-natured person. My voice is gentle. The ugly noise that shows up in my head belongs to someone else. Likewise, the unloving voice in your head is not yours. It has been planted there by people and experiences that were painful. It is your duty to yourself to reject that voice entirely so you can benefit from the same loving kindness you offer others.

## Takeaways and Talking Points

+ The voice in your head is a compilation of the many voices you have heard throughout your life.

+ Your inner critic is born from your painful experiences. Your brain developed that voice to keep you from experiencing failure and rejection out in the world. Unfortunately for many, that voice gets out of control.

+ To achieve self-love, you must learn to quiet your inner critic and find your original, true voice. This is the voice of encouragement, enthusiasm, and wisdom that has always been inside you.

## Pack Your Self-Love Suitcase
## with Self-Kindness

The first item you'll need to bring on your self-love journey is self-kindness. Critical self-talk is fatal to self-love. Gentle, friendly self-talk is the foundation on which self-love is built. Although speaking to yourself with kindness may feel unnatural and even silly in the beginning, each time you engage in it, you are priming your brain to be more open and accepting of self-kindness. Ultimately, it will feel natural and healing to speak to yourself this way, and you will be ready to continue on your journey toward self-love.

# Chapter Two

# Developing Self-Compassion

*Self-compassion is simply
giving the same kindness to ourselves
that we would give to others.*

—Christopher Germer

The primary reason it is easier to offer kindness to others when they struggle is that we connect with compassion for them. If a friend tells you they are struggling in school, you take all the other factors of their life into consideration. Maybe they also work a full-time job. Perhaps they have stress in their romantic or family life. Their professor could have a reputation for being cantankerous, or maybe they are having financial difficulties. You examine all the burdens they carry and offer empathy for their hardships. You can understand why they are struggling the way they are because of the other circumstances occurring in their life. However, it can be challenging to be as objective when examining your own difficulties.

A key component of self-love is learning how to practice self-compassion. We must learn to step outside our struggles and see them in the context of the rest of our lives. Often, our present-day hardships were set up for us many years prior. To highlight this, let's examine the story of a young woman named Nyah.

✦ ✦ ✦

## Nyah's Story

"Nyah" was raised by her grandparents after her drug-addicted parents abandoned her. Her grandparents were financially secure but were hoarders. In addition to living in crowded, unsanitary conditions, they hoarded their money. Nyah knew her grandparents loved her, but they did not have the emotional well-being to care for a young child. As a result, many of Nyah's needs were not met. She was often not permitted to eat enough for a growing child because her grandmother didn't want to spend too much money on food. Her grandmother took her to secondhand stores to buy clothes and made Nyah choose items that were several sizes too big so she could grow into them. Nyah felt as though she "looked like a clown" at school and struggled to fit in and make friends.

Every so often, Nyah would spend time with her other set of grandparents. They were wealthy and lived a lavish lifestyle. While her everyday life was lonely and dreary, this alternate life seemed magical. This set of grandparents lived in a beautiful home, drove luxury cars, and wore designer clothes. They occasionally swooped into Nyah's life and showered her with presents, vacations, and fancy meals at expensive restaurants. Then they plopped her back into her real life.

Precious Nyah, with her young, undeveloped brain, grappled to make sense of her challenging daily life and the fairy-tale life she occasionally experienced. Without healthy adult guidance, she concluded on her own that money equated to happiness. People with money, who wore nice clothes and lived in big houses and went on glamourous vacations, were happy. People like her, who lived like paupers, were sad, friendless, and unworthy.

As Nyah grew into adulthood, she became obsessed with image management. She was embarrassed by her grandparents, her home, her clothes, and her life. She got a job in high school so she could buy her own clothes, makeup, and hair products. She made every effort to be perceived by others as beautiful, successful, and likable. Since she never learned how to establish and maintain friendships appropriately, she believed her likability was based on what others thought of her and in what she could offer them.

Nyah was repeatedly taken advantage of by friends and romantic partners because she allowed herself to be used. She often paid the entire bill when she went out for dinner with a group. She took her girlfriends shopping and treated them to pedicures to entice them to spend time with her. She did not honor her body in romantic relationships. She was sexual with men sooner than she wanted because she was so afraid to say no and displease them. For Nyah, nothing was worse than rejection. She was willing to do virtually anything to avoid being seen as unlovable.

By the time Nyah went to therapy, her preoccupation with "looking perfect" was ruining her life. She spent so much time hyperfocusing on appearing "good enough" that she didn't have any idea who she was. Nyah tried desperately to be likable and thought emulating the seemingly happy life of her wealthy grandparents would bring her the happiness she desired. She believed she had failed because she was as lonely and unhappy as ever. Stuck in her childlike way of thinking, she was convinced that if she could just get the next big thing, a new car, a breast augmentation, the right shoes, hang with a more successful crowd, then she might finally achieve happiness. Though this way of living failed her time and again, she was stuck thinking she was unhappy because she had not yet reached a high enough status. She could not shift her thinking to realize the external things she obsessed over were never going to bring her happiness.

✦ ✦ ✦

It was clear that Nyah did not love herself. Through the objective eyes of another, it was easy to understand why. Nyah was smart, beautiful, creative, talented, and kind. She was lovable in every way, but a childhood marked by abandonment and solitude left her brutally scarred with insecurity and self-loathing. This is a common psychological phenomenon. When a person endures a childhood of physical or emotional deprivation, they often grow into adults who yearn for more and more, never feeling satiated. Nyah yearned for love and belonging, friendship, acceptance, and validation. Unfortunately, because she felt so unworthy in her core, no amount of external affirmation could satisfy her needs.

It was initially difficult for Nyah to see that her feelings of inadequacy were not based in reality but rather in painful childhood experiences. Nyah's journey to wellness required her to go back in time and connect with the little girl she once was. Once she reframed her self-doubt as fear brought up by that lonely little girl, she softened toward herself and responded to her insecurity with gentle kindness. It was the development of self-compassion that ultimately allowed Nyah to shift the way she saw herself and her life.

In time, Nyah learned to intervene on her distorted beliefs. When the thought *You had better say yes, or he won't like you* popped into her head, she recognized it as the voice of a scared, unhappy girl who was abandoned by her parents to live in disarray with mentally unfit grandparents. She learned to embrace the little-girl part of herself with the compassion of a wise, understanding adult. She engaged in compassionate dialogue with herself to challenge her old belief systems.

Eventually, Nyah started to see herself the way she truly was: a bright, thoughtful, funny, delightful young woman who deserved much more than the people in her early life gave her. She came to see that, had the adults in her life done right by her, she would not have believed herself to be unworthy or unlovable. In a different childhood, Nyah might have grown to see herself as capable, worthy, and lovable because that was the truth. This realization was unexpected and life-changing for Nyah. She was not unworthy or unlovable. Her difficult childhood experiences imprinted her with lies about herself and the world that she needed to unlearn.

Over time, the intentional practice of self-compassion allowed Nyah to see herself through loving eyes. She transformed her unkind inner voice into one that was empathic, gentle, and empowering. As she came to understand her worthiness and lovability, she recognized that she deserved happiness. Nyah learned that being herself was enough. She didn't have to prove herself to others to earn their affection; she already deserved it for just being her. Nyah became a fierce defender and protector of the insecure little-girl part of her. She no longer tolerated others using or disrespecting her. This created a freedom Nyah had never known and allowed her to find herself, be true to herself, and insist that people in her life treat her the way she deserved to be treated. It was a beautiful transformation.

## Self-Kindness

Dr. Kristin Neff is a leading psychologist in the realm of self-compassion. Her book, *Self-Compassion: The Proven Power of Being Kind to Yourself*, was one of the most inspirational reads of my life. In it, Dr. Neff describes three elements of self-compassion: self-kindness, a sense of common humanity, and mindfulness. Regarding self-kindness, she writes, "Self-compassion entails being warm and understanding toward ourselves when we suffer, fail, or feel inadequate, rather than ignoring our pain or flagellating ourselves with self-criticism." When we understand and expect that failure is a natural part of life, we reduce the suffering we experience during periods of disappointment through self-directed gentleness and acceptance. Self-kindness can make us more likely to try again or find another way to persevere because kindness is encouraging. It builds our resiliency and belief in ourselves instead of discouraging and breaking us down.

## Sense of Common Humanity

The next key component involves connecting yourself to a sense of common humanity. This practice allows us to acknowledge that pain and feelings of inadequacy are something all humans experience. We often feel isolated and alone in our burdens. Remembering that our struggles are part of what connects us to all other people can help ease our pain and normalize our experiences. Instead of berating yourself, try saying, "I struggle because I am human. Part of the human experience is to feel alone, unsure, and inadequate at times. But I am not alone. My battle to overcome insecurity is one of the things that connects me to all other people. I am imperfect just like everyone else." This type of inner dialogue will help you feel normal rather than isolated and inadequate when you experience pain.

# Mindfulness

Finally, we can't adequately practice self-compassion without a mindfulness practice. Dr. Neff writes, "Mindfulness is a non-judgmental, receptive mind state in which one observes thoughts and feelings as they are, without trying to suppress or deny them." Essentially, mindfulness allows us to observe our thoughts and feelings without attaching to them as fact. When we are open and curious about our internal experiences, we can view them more objectively, without minimizing or exaggerating them.

Practicing the three components of self-compassion is a great way to begin a practice of self-love, but I don't want to oversimplify this process. Self-compassion is a challenge for many people. Trauma survivors often have a difficult time shifting from self-loathing to self-compassion. Some find it intolerable to speak kindly to themselves in the beginning. Self-compassion requires practice and patience. You wouldn't expect to speak fluent Mandarin after one lesson, and you can't expect to be fluent in self-compassion after one lesson either.

Even those who do not consider themselves trauma survivors struggle with this concept. Many of the thought and behavior changes suggested in this book will feel quite unnatural in the beginning. That's expected. Your brain learned to perform in a certain way, and you have repeatedly reinforced that way of thinking. Anything that contradicts the way you've been thinking and behaving your whole life will feel "wrong" at first. Eventually, it will begin to feel healthy and right to be kind to yourself. Before we get ahead of ourselves, though, let's spend a little more time exploring why your brain became locked into being unkind to itself in the first place.

## Takeaways and Talking Points

✦ Your painful, early life experiences contribute to the negative beliefs you hold about yourself in adulthood.

✦ A self-compassion practice encourages you to treat yourself with kindness and give yourself the same grace you give others.

✦ Practicing self-compassion is foundational in quieting your inner critic and engaging in more positive, realistic self-talk.

✦ When you engage in self-compassion, you reassure yourself with the same empathy and understanding you offer to those you love.

## Pack Your Self-Love Suitcase with Self-Acceptance

We all have parts of ourselves and our stories that we hide from others. It's natural to feel insecure, afraid, and even ashamed. But when we replace those feelings with self-acceptance, we move closer to self-love. We must find empathy for ourselves in our story. Self-acceptance allows us to step outside ourselves and see a bigger picture, one that includes understanding for what we are going through and compassion for our struggle. When we stop judging ourselves and start accepting ourselves, we make space for our feelings, our responses, and our shortcomings. True self-love requires acceptance of our whole self and our whole story, not just the parts we feel good about.

# CHAPTER THREE

# The Journey Back to Your Original Self

*If you want others to be happy,*
*practice compassion.*
*If you want to be happy,*
*practice compassion.*

—Dalai Lama XIV

Sometimes when people first begin therapy, they ask, "Why am I struggling with this?" As humans, we struggle in various ways, and often people don't understand why they are plagued by their particular problems. Why alcohol? Why rage? Why overeating, online gambling, or commitment issues? In all my years of practice, I never met a person whose problem was coincidental. Every person I met followed a specific life path that led them to a unique set of challenges that made complete sense once they unpacked their history.

I often tell clients that therapy is a journey back to your original self, back to the person you were before life's hardships got in the way and changed the trajectory of who you would become. In my practice,

I have had the honor to work alongside Marilyn Murray, a brilliant mental health professional. During her work as a therapist, Marilyn developed a theory and wrote a book titled *The Murray Method*, which conceptualizes the impact of early life trauma on adult behavior. She coined the term *original child* to describe the person you are at birth. This is your original self, with all your innate talents, positive attributes, and capabilities. This person has the potential to grow up into the best possible version of you.

If life is exceptionally kind to you, you could, in theory, walk a straight line from your original self to your best adult self. I have never met a person who walked that straight line. Perhaps those unicorns are out there, but I don't know any. And here you are reading a book about how to love yourself, so I'm guessing you're no unicorn either. All the people I have ever known, myself included, walked a crooked path that was shifted continuously by the uncontrollable circumstances of their lives. At some point in the journey, we all stopped and said to ourselves, "Wait a minute, what am I doing? How did I get here?" We realized we veered far from the path we started on. We moved in a direction farther and farther away from our original selves, from our best selves.

We all come to a juncture where we need to make a choice. Do I stay on this course? Do I continue to be impacted by my past and let my painful life experiences define how I see myself and how I interact with the world? Or do I turn around, find the person I once was, and nurture all the potential inside me so I can be my happiest, healthiest self? In my own journey, the answer was clear. I reached a juncture and knew it was time to turn around. And for you, well, you are here, so you must be ready to turn around, too. Let's look at another case example to identify how this process of "losing yourself" through your life experiences unfolds.

✦ ✦ ✦

# Daniel's Story

"Daniel" started therapy at his wife's request. She was frustrated with Daniel's quick temper and was often embarrassed by him in public. She described situations in which he would snap at a waiter or customer service person in ways that seemed completely unreasonable for the situation. The last straw came when they were on vacation and Daniel flipped out because the jacuzzi tub in their suite did not work. He called the front desk, irate, proclaiming he had paid extra for a jacuzzi and demanding the hotel not only move them to a room with a working tub but also provide additional upgrades for the inconvenience. His wife could not understand why her typically kind and rational husband got so enraged and demanding over minor inconveniences most others would accept as a normal part of life and handle in stride.

This pattern of behavior created a strain on their relationship, and Daniel was finally ready to make a change. He recognized that he went from zero to a hundred in a moment but did not understand why. He agreed to explore his life story to find the answer.

Daniel grew up with an alcoholic mother and an abusive step-father. His mother was loving but did not protect her son in the face of her husband's violence. Instead, she drank to numb the pain of her husband's abuse and effectively left her son to fend for himself. It was confusing for Daniel to grow up in a home where he had a caring parent who was attentive to him in many ways but who also permitted abuse to be perpetrated upon him.

As he unpacked his childhood experiences, Daniel came to understand that he was traumatized by his mother just as much as by his stepfather. The physical and emotional abuse perpetrated by his step-father was damaging in many ways, especially to his self-esteem. However, it was the dynamic of having a loving but unprotective mother that made him hypersensitive to any perceived injustice. Daniel could not wrap his mind around how his mother could so clearly love him and still fail to care for his safety in the most basic and critical ways. There was something so wrong, so unjust about it that, as he grew, he became acutely aware of injustices around him and fiercely fought back against them. Of course, much of this was below his conscious level of awareness, but as he progressed in therapy, it became clear to him. He was unable to protect himself as a child, and because his mother had not protected him, he developed a strong need in adulthood to defend himself in any circumstance that seemed unfair.

✦ ✦ ✦

Without realizing it, Daniel was attaching his abusive stepfather's face to people he encountered in his adult life. If a customer service person accidentally rang up an item without giving him the marked sale price, Daniel's internal alarms went off. He perceived the person as maliciously trying to do him wrong. Daniel was triggered. His trigger point was specific to his life experience. If you were to watch him berate a customer service person for trying to "cheat" him out of the sale price, he would appear unreasonable and unhinged. However, if you examined his behavior in the context of his life experiences, it made perfect sense.

Once Daniel made the connection between his childhood experience and his unhelpful adult behavior, he began to intervene on himself when he was triggered. He learned to gently reassure that young part of himself. He developed a kind inner voice that said things like,

"This person is not like my stepfather. They are not trying to hurt me. I'm just triggered because I am reminded of a time when someone was trying to hurt me, and I could not protect myself. I can protect myself today, and I can do it with grace and composure. I don't need to fight. I don't need to explode. I can advocate for myself appropriately because the person I am dealing with today does not have cruel intentions. They will help me resolve the issue if I stay calm."

Over time, Daniel retrained his brain using a compassionate inner voice. By speaking to himself from a place of kindness and understanding, Daniel settled his strong emotional reactions. Eventually, his responses to perceived injustices became less and less reactive. Before he had this level of self-awareness, he could not explain his reactivity to his wife.

### Shame

Daniel's wife experienced him as ridiculous when he was triggered and would tell him so. As unhealthy as Daniel's behavior was, when his wife said, "You're acting like a crazy person. You need to calm the hell down," she wasn't helping the situation. She was shaming him when he was in a vulnerable emotional state.

Daniel also shamed himself for his behavior, telling himself, "This is idiotic. What's wrong with me? I should be able to manage minor stressors without flying off the handle." Daniel felt remorse, but he was not going to resolve his problematic behavior through shaming. He needed to understand why he was reacting the way he was, so he could come alongside that young part of him from a place of adult wisdom. It was only through compassionate understanding and a kind internal dialogue that Daniel was able to give up his unhealthy responses and develop healthy alternative behavior using self-love.

# Healing from Childhood Struggles

First, you must understand the origins of your unique struggle. Once you understand why you think and behave the way you do, the real work begins. With your newfound understanding, you must shift into compassion and intervene kindly on yourself. This is where the process can get tricky. It is easy to say, "Just be kind to yourself!" It's hard to actually do it. Part of the difficulty lies in the disconnect that often exists between your adult identity and your child identity. You might say, "Well sure, I understand why that little kid was struggling, but I'm an adult now. I should know better!"

### *"Should" Is a Dangerous Word*

We tell ourselves we "should" know a lot of things we don't know. We should just get over it, or we should behave differently than we do. We "should" know better. But should we? Based on everything we learned about ourselves and the world from our early life experiences, we may or may not know things that would be helpful. Age itself is not a reason one should be expected to know something. We can't possibly know things that have not been properly taught to and engrained in us. No amount of aging will magically teach us what we need to know to be our best selves. We must have adequate learning experiences. Without proper teaching, there is no way to expect that anyone should understand something, no matter how old they are.

Perhaps a fifteen-year-old "should" be able to read. But if a fifteen-year-old grew up in a remote tribal village without Westernized schooling, how could he be expected to be literate? Maybe a twenty-five-year-old "should" know how to file her taxes. The truth is, she may or may not know how to file them depending on what she has been taught about managing her finances. The same rings true for how we respond to stress, deal with conflict, manage our emotions, and handle our interpersonal relationships. We only know what we have learned, and we can't possibly know what we haven't learned. We can criticize ourselves and one another for not knowing what we "should" already know, but we will never shame ourselves into learning anything.

Maya Angelou said it perfectly: "Do the best you can until you know better. When you know better, do better." The only way we can expect ourselves or anyone else to be proficient at anything is through learned experiences. When we have trouble with something, it is simply because we have not yet had enough opportunity to practice and become proficient.

For example, you could argue that we "should" all know that eating a pint of ice cream when you are sad is not the most helpful thing to do. But if in childhood you did not have a healthy adult to adequately teach you how to identify upset feelings and self-soothe in constructive ways, you might have had to figure it out yourself. A child has minimal capabilities for determining how to regulate distressing emotions without the guidance of an emotionally intelligent and responsive adult. And guess what? Eating feels good. Eating ice cream feels really good. If a child is left alone to determine how to soothe their distressing emotions, they might just discover that eating sweets works.

Further, it is likely they will carry their unhealthy coping strategy into adulthood if they are not presented with adequate tools for coping in healthier ways. Simply learning that sweets aren't good for you or hearing that emotional eating is "bad" isn't going to somehow instill healthier coping methods. When you're hurting, you're going to go back to the self-soothing tool you know works, even if it has negative repercussions.

## The Power of Reparenting

This is where the concept of "reparenting" comes in. When we begin our journey back to our original selves, parts of us are disjointed. We have a young, unresolved, broken part of us and a wiser, adult part of us. These parts need to be integrated. Once we identify our triggers and can see our unhealthy behavior for what it is, we need to "reparent" that young part of us. We must provide for ourselves what we needed back then that was unavailable.

In my earlier example, Daniel needed to honor the young part of him that was helpless and needed protection. He learned to advocate for himself without letting the kid in him lash out. It took much more than merely saying, "An adult should know not to overreact to minor inconveniences." Daniel needed more profound understanding about why he behaved the way he did, so he could (1) recognize his triggers, (2) heal his wounded parts, and (3) reparent himself. Only through repeated and reinforced experiences was he finally able to respond appropriately (instead of reactively) in situations that felt unfair. It took learning and practice before his new, healthy behavior was instinctive.

Likewise, if your issue is emotional eating, you must learn to provide comfort to yourself in ways that are effective and permanently healing. That tub of Rocky Road is just a Band-Aid for your painful feelings. It makes sense that you turned to food if using food for comfort was modeled in your home, or if no solutions for self-soothing were taught to you at all. Your job now is to be the stronger, wiser adult figure for that little kid you once were. You must learn to say to yourself, "I know this is hard. This hurts. Eating ice cream might mask that pain for a short time, but it won't solve the problem. I can figure out what I really need to fix this."

Clearly, eating a pint of ice cream is not the most loving way to treat yourself. Though it may temporarily feel good, it will likely be followed by more intense negative feelings such as shame, hopelessness, or self-loathing. Acting with self-love often means not acting on what feels best in the moment. Sometimes the most self-loving thing you can do is something you don't want to do at all. It might be calling a friend and asking for help. It could be getting out of bed and going to the store or the gym or anywhere just to get out of your house and interact with people. The most self-loving thing might be challenging yourself to do what you are most afraid of, like leaning into your social anxiety by signing up for a dance class or volunteering at an animal shelter. Let me drive this message home by telling you about James and how he learned to reparent himself.

✦ ✦ ✦

## James's Story

The purpose of reparenting is to guide yourself with love and wisdom while instituting the boundaries and limitations a healthy adult would impose on a child they are raising. "James" had a mother who was obsessed with her weight and projected her fear of becoming overweight onto all her children. She restricted their food intake and labeled foods as "good" or "bad." As a child, James longed for sweets but was not allowed to have them. His mother wouldn't let him have second helpings when he asked for them for fear he would "get fat." In adolescence, he began to rebel against his restrictive mother. He would buy and hide candy bars and chips. He would eat several servings at a time in hiding.

This behavior carried into adulthood. James didn't initially see his behavior as an act of rebellion against his mother. However, once he connected to the young part of himself, he saw how hiding food was the way he exercised self-agency to meet his needs. James utilized reparenting techniques to regulate his consumption of sweets from a grounded place. He didn't need to eat two candy bars in his car on the way home from work. He certainly could. He was an adult now, free to make his own choices. He no longer had to live under his mother's rules. He came to see he didn't really want or need two candy bars after work. He just wanted to feel free to make his own choices and not be controlled by others.

James learned to reparent himself from a wise, loving place. When he felt an urge to eat in hiding, he said to himself, "Am I really hungry? If so, what healthy choices can I make to nourish my body? Maybe I feel out of control and am looking for a way to take my power back. What situation in my life is causing this feeling? How can I deal with the issue directly to restore my sense of control over my life?"

James changed his relationship with food. He learned to say to himself, "I can choose to eat whatever I want, whenever I want. I have freedom and self-agency today that I didn't have when I was a kid. I like my adult freedom. I also value my health, and I love myself enough to nourish my body with healthy foods most of the time and treat myself on occasion." As a child, James needed an adult who could teach him about healthy eating without being unreasonable and restrictive. He didn't have that then, but with time and effort, he became that person for himself in adulthood.

Reparenting is a process—in the same way that learning to speak a new language or play an instrument is a process. The lessons must be repeated and practiced before they become second nature. Just because you are an adult doesn't mean you should expect yourself to get it and change your old patterns instantly. Once the brain has learned how to do something one way, it takes effort and consistency to retrain that thought process. If you have been doing something one way for many years (even if it has been ineffective), you can't possibly expect your brain to just switch over at a moment's notice. You will have to utilize patience, understanding, and love as you teach yourself a better way of being.

## Takeaways and Talking Points

+ The things you struggle with in adulthood are often directly correlated to your early life experiences. They are not a representation of your innate defectiveness. Rather, they reflect childhood difficulties you never fully resolved.

+ Reparenting is a technique you can utilize to resolve the issues from your youth that create problems in your adult life. This mindset allows you to make sense of your struggles without being hard on yourself. Instead, you can approach yourself with kindness, and use your adult wisdom to grow underdeveloped parts of you.

+ Reparenting doesn't just mean loving the younger parts of yourself. It also means instituting the healthy boundaries and accountability that a loving adult imposes on their children.

## Pack Your Self-Love Suitcase
## with Self-Parenting

Setting boundaries with yourself is an act of self-love. In the same way a loving parent nurtures, guides, and teaches a child, we must be the adult our younger selves needed. Self-parenting allows us to integrate self-kindness and self-acceptance with healthy self-imposed boundaries so we can be the best version of ourselves. Loving parents don't let their kids do whatever they want, whenever they want. Boundaries say, "I love you and I want what is best for you, even if it means making a tough choice right now." That's why self-parenting is so important on the path to self-love.

## Chapter Four

# Loving Your Inner Child

*You've been criticizing yourself for*
*years and it hasn't worked.*
*Try approving of yourself and*
*see what happens.*

—Louise L. Hay

I work at a practice in Scottsdale, Arizona, called Psychological Counseling Services (PCS). We are a large practice of over twenty psychologists and therapists who work as a team in an intensive outpatient treatment setting where people come from all over the world to receive sixty hours of therapy in a week's time. Our primary focus is on treating issues around addiction and unresolved trauma.

As you may imagine, for a person to decide they need sixty hours of therapy in a week, their life must be pretty out of control. Usually, clients come to us in a state of crisis because their lives have become unmanageable. They are often at a critical point in decision making. Maybe they have just lost a job or are trying to avoid divorce. Whatever the reason, they are usually ready to take drastic steps to turn their lives around.

## Connecting to Your Original Self

One of our primary treatment objectives is to help clients identify, connect to, and begin loving their original selves. We offer many therapeutic interventions to achieve this. My favorite might be the stuffed animal assignment. We send clients to a store at the mall where people (often children) go to construct a stuffed animal of their choosing. We send our adult clients there to build a representation of their inner child.

When I assign this exercise to clients, it is often met with hesitation. Men especially feel embarrassed at the idea of going alone into a store for children to make a stuffed animal. I explain that the purpose of the exercise is to connect to the original part of themselves before shame or embarrassment even existed. I ask clients to capture the essence of the child they once were. I instruct them to think about what they were like before the hardships of life imprinted on them. I ask them, "What did you like about that little person?" I get responses like, "She was happy. She liked herself. She was carefree. She liked to get messy and didn't care how she looked." I also hear, "He was curious. He liked to build things. He was creative and sensitive. He was fun." Holding those attributes in mind, clients are instructed to make a stuffed animal that represents those wonderful qualities they once embodied in their unadulterated form.

When the assignment is complete, they bring their creation back to my office and introduce it to me. I have seen everything from a koala in a sparkling tutu to a monkey wearing fishing garb to a teddy bear in pajamas. I love hearing the experiences people have as they work to remember their young selves and connect to their innate goodness. Even the most hesitant clients often come back proud of their stuffed animals. I encourage them to keep them in a place where they can see them every day and recall the little person they once were. More important, I ask them to remember their ongoing commitment to honor and protect the young part of themselves.

I like to share a favorite Sonny Melendrez quote that goes, "You are every age you ever were." I ask them to remember that there is still a five-year-old part of themselves, a ten-year-old, an angsty teenager, a hopeful twenty-something, and so on and so forth. We cannot discard all these younger versions of ourselves. They are still alive inside us and have needs the current versions of us must attend to. If you are to become your best self, you must be connected to your original self. Only then can you grow that young person into the adult you wish to be.

Now it's your turn. I invite you to design your own inner child representation. Get creative with it. Have fun. Look, if going to the mall isn't your jam, go to your local craft store and make something out of fabric, wood, or paper. Pull out your old photos or scrapbooks for inspiration. Really try to recall what it was like being that small person. I want you to remember everything funny, precious, and special about young you. Imagine who you might have become if those qualities were fully nurtured. Who might you be today if your painful life experiences hadn't disrupted your natural blossoming? Sometimes this is hard to envision. Let me share Ling's story with you to illuminate the process.

## Ling's Story

"Ling" struggled with the stuffed animal assignment because she did not like her young self very much. She came to therapy because drug abuse had taken over her life. She had tried to get sober many times. She had been to rehab more than once but couldn't stay clean. For Ling, getting high allowed her to escape a sense of self-loathing that was intolerable when she was sober.

As she shared her life story in therapy, Ling recounted her childhood experience as a young girl with severe learning disabilities. She was reared in a Chinese-American home of high achievers. Both her parents had master's degrees, and they ran a successful business together. She was the youngest of four children. The family expectation was for all the children to be straight-A students. High marks came easy for Ling's three older siblings. Such was not the case for Ling.

Ling remembered sitting in class, watching the teacher work on the board, and not understanding a thing. She felt confused and frightened by her lack of comprehension. She observed that other children easily grasped the concepts she struggled to understand. Ling felt overwhelmed and full of shame. Initially, she tried to elicit help from her parents and older siblings but was met with annoyance. Her parents showed little patience for her struggle and made quips like, "This is so easy. How do you not understand this?" They accused her of not applying herself and being "lazy." Her siblings were outright cruel, calling her "stupid" and "retarded." She soon learned she would not get her needs met from her family.

In school, Ling worked hard to hide her struggles. She paid attention as best she could and pretended to know what was going on. Reading was especially difficult. She attended elementary school in an age before learning disabilities were as quickly identified and treated as they are today. It wasn't until she was twelve years old that she was diagnosed with dyslexia. By that time, considerable damage had already been done. Her diagnosis provided an explanation but didn't change her deeply ingrained perception of herself as "stupid." Even with intervention, Ling continued to struggle, knowing she was different from her siblings and peers. She saw her learning disability as proof that she was innately defective.

Ling compared herself constantly to her older siblings, especially a sister who was only one year her senior but who seemingly excelled in everything she did. Her sister enjoyed praise and acclamation from friends, teachers, and, most important, her parents. While her parents became more tolerant of Ling's academic struggles, they never seemed to show her the pride they did for their other children. As a result, Ling felt "less than" in every way.

One thing Ling had was incredible artistic talent. She drew magnificently and longed for other creative opportunities such as painting and mixed media projects. Unfortunately, because her parents did not value art as a skill that could be readily monetized, her artistic talents were not appropriately nurtured. Ling always felt like a square peg being forced into a round hole. She just couldn't fit into the expectations her family created for her.

By the time Ling reached adolescence, her sense of self was built entirely around her belief that she was "stupid" and "different." She felt like a failure. Because her artistic talents had not been celebrated by her parents, she found little comfort in her skills. She longed for solace and was vulnerable to anything that would take away her pain, no matter how destructive. Ling was only eleven years old when she started drinking alcohol and thirteen the first time she smoked marijuana. By her sophomore year of high school, she was using heroin.

Ling's self-esteem only got worse because of her drug use. She put herself in dangerous situations, worried her parents half to death, and lost all connection to her siblings in the years that led to her first intervention. She stole from her parents to get drug money, disappeared for days and weeks at a time, and experienced a multitude of drug-related traumas in her early twenties, including being arrested twice and raped on multiple occasions. Ling was trapped in a vicious cycle of hating herself, gaining temporary relief through substance use, and then hating herself even more because of the choices she made under the influence of drugs. The only way she knew to escape her pain was with narcotics, but using inevitably brought her more pain.

When Ling finally achieved a period of sustained sobriety, she was overwhelmed by self-loathing. She explained that substance treatment and twelve-step programs were inadequate in keeping her clean because her sober life was so painful. She was burdened by years of self-hatred from childhood. Piled onto that were years of guilt over poor choices that hurt her and her family. Her parents weren't perfect, but they loved her, and she felt they did not deserve what she had put them through.

✦ ✦ ✦

This brings us back to Ling's stuffed animal assignment. Ling didn't like her young self. Her younger self was "stupid" in her eyes. She felt if that little girl she was hadn't been so inadequate, she would not have suffered the painful existence that was her life. She had no compassion for that little girl. Moreover, she resented her.

Ling needed to go back in time, way back, to a time before her learning disability disrupted her life. She needed to find the playful little girl who loved art. She had to see the happy child who carted her paper and colored pencils outside to draw trees and flowers. Ling needed connection with the girl who sat at the kitchen table drawing pictures of herself having fantastic adventures. Finally, Ling's search for her original child led to a breakthrough. She recalled a drawing she once made of herself on the top of Mount Everest. "There was a time I thought I could do anything. I believed in myself then."

Ling discovered the purest version of herself. She saw a child who was smart, creative, and gentle. Once she remembered the little girl who felt capable, likable, and deserving of love and happiness, she realized she was still all those things. Ling embarked on a rescue mission: a mission to save a child with a learning disability who was mismanaged by the adults in her life.

Through the empathy she developed for that little girl, Ling was able to see that had her learning disability been diagnosed early and then normalized and validated, she might have had a different outcome. If the people in her life had been compassionate and understanding, she might have learned to love herself despite her challenges. Had her strengths been acknowledged and nurtured, she might have built her identity around her talents instead of hyperfocusing on her weaknesses.

Ling was a bright, tenderhearted child with an artistic mind that worked differently than the norm. That made her unique and brought her special gifts. Those gifts should have been celebrated. They weren't, and that wasn't her fault. She deserved better than what the adults in her life gave her. This insight brought her both empathy for the little girl she was and resentment toward the adults who failed her. As is often the case in self-discovery and emotional healing, completing one piece of work can lead to another part that needs to be resolved.

## Takeaways and Talking Points

+ Painful childhood experiences imprint us with inaccurate beliefs about ourselves.

+ To free yourself from a negative self-image, you must find and rescue the original version of you.

+ Your mission is to love and nurture your younger self so you can grow into the healthy adult you are meant to be.

+ It can be helpful to create a tangible representation of your young self to keep focused on your mission. Get creative and make a piece of art that embodies the essence of the child you once were.

## Pack Your Self-Love Suitcase with Self-Commitment

As you continue collecting the tools you need on your self-love journey, you must include self-commitment. You've begun making connections to your past trauma and your current struggles. It's time to commit yourself to that young person. You can do them justice by making decisions today that are in their best interest and, in turn, are in your best interest. When we love the child we were and refuse to abandon them any longer, it's easier to love and be committed to our well-being today.

## Chapter Five

# The Gift of Forgiveness

*Forgiveness does not change the past,*
*but it does enlarge the future.*

—Paul Lewis Boese

In the last example, Ling's journey led her to an unexpected juncture. She knew she was angry at herself when she entered treatment. As she began to connect to her inner child and started loving herself, she realized she was upset with her parents, too. But before she could shift into forgiveness, Ling needed to come to terms with her natural, appropriate feelings of anger.

So many of us are afraid to express any anger toward our parents. Many were reared with phrases like "Don't argue with me," or "Zip your lip!" When you have been raised to accept your parents' words as the be-all and end-all, it's no wonder you feel you don't have the right to be angry with your parents for anything.

The truth is, parents make mistakes all the time, and it's okay for young children and adult children to sometimes feel angry toward their parents. If we are determined to be emotionally whole adults, we need to learn how to feel, appropriately express, and resolve our anger. You can't rush forgiveness. It isn't that simple. True forgiveness can only come once hurt and anger have been adequately reconciled.

That said, forgiveness is one of the most constructive, freeing gifts we can give ourselves. Anger and resentment can devour us. They keep us stuck and give our power away to the person or thing we have anger toward. Author Malachy McCourt said, "Resentment is like taking poison and waiting for the other person to die." Nothing festers, rots, and destroys our happiness more than anger and resentment. The act of forgiveness, whether toward ourselves or others, is a gift that frees our spirits, unburdens our hearts, and allows us to live the life we deserve despite the painful experiences we have lived through.

You and I, we've been working on this relationship for the past several chapters. You came to me in your time of need, and change takes trust. But trust is a two-way street. Now I want to tell you part of my own story. I am sharing my deeply personal experience with you because I want you to know that I get it. I know how much it takes to trust yourself and to trust this process. I'm not a psychologist sitting on my armchair like it's a throne, professing to be perfect or all-knowing. I've screwed up more times than I could ever recount. In fact, I've screwed things up so monumentally, so many times, that I've finally gotten good at the repair and recover part. I still screw up. I can still be selfish, ignorant, and unreasonable. I hurt people I love, and they hurt me. That's real life.

This brings us to my story. I had to master forgiveness if I wanted to be truly happy. I have been both the adult child who needed to forgive parents who failed me and the parent who failed. Without a doubt, the greatest gift I ever gave myself was making amends to my eldest daughter and forgiving myself for how I let her down.

# Heidi's Story

I was just fifteen years old when I got pregnant for the first time. Although I won't detail all the dysfunctional family dynamics that led me at fifteen to look for love and affirmation outside my family, they were significant. My mother was loving but she was an alcoholic. My parents divorced when I was four years old, and my mom married an abusive and volatile man. Outside holidays and summer vacations, my father's presence was nonexistent during my young life because he moved halfway across the country. I was in a lot of pain as a child and adolescent.

As is the case in many families, my parents made a lot of mistakes but were good people. In an act of redemption, when they learned I was pregnant, they offered to help in every way they could as I raised my child. Twenty-one days after my Sweet Sixteen birthday, my precious daughter was born.

Alex became the light of my life. She was pure and beautiful. She needed me as much as I needed her. Caring for her gave me purpose and a sense of unconditional love I had not yet known. That was a responsibility no newborn should carry. It was not her job to make me feel loved and important. It was my job to bestow those gifts upon her. I really tried. I got up at night to give her bottles. I awoke in the dark of early morning to take her to day care before I went to high school. I held her, kissed her, read to her, and played with her in between doing my homework and trying to be an ordinary sixteen-year-old. I, too, did my best.

Unfortunately for Alex, my best was sometimes just not good enough. I couldn't care for myself at sixteen, so I often failed in caring for her. She was a colicky baby who needed extra love and attention.

Sometimes she needed more than I had to give. I got frustrated. I became exhausted from hours of walking and bouncing her to soothe her upset tummy. I sometimes let her "cry it out" in her electronic baby swing when I couldn't take the responsibility anymore.

I knew nothing of child development. My dad bragged about how he trained me to sleep through the night as an infant by ignoring the cries and screams from my crib. I didn't know what "crying it out" did to an infant's developing brain. My parents didn't know either. I know now that allowing a baby to cry alone for long periods teaches them they cannot get their needs met. It can make them anxious and untrusting. It interferes with their ability to self-soothe. I wish I knew that then. I made so many mistakes with lasting consequences.

The reality was, we lived in a highly dysfunctional household. I did not have the power at sixteen to shield Alex from all the unhealthy dynamics that existed. I was tired and overwhelmed and a naturally self-centered adolescent. Try as I might, there was only so much I had to give. I knew I needed to get out of my family home as soon as I could, but my self-esteem was abysmal. I doubted my ability to find love or care for myself independently.

Truth be told, I put far too much weight on the importance of finding a partner. I wish I had the gift of feminism back then so I could have seen myself as powerful and capable, independent of a romantic relationship. Such was not my life at the time. I thought the best I could hope for was to marry a nice man who would take good care of me. I felt like damaged goods, and my expectations for myself and my life were woefully low. When I was twenty years old, I married the older brother of a high school friend, not so much for love but for security. I had always envied my friend for her loving family. I wanted Alex to be part of a "good family," too.

I was married for nearly seven years and had two other daughters with my first husband before we divorced. It was a tumultuous marriage from the beginning, and had it not been for my deep insecurities, it would never have lasted as long as it did. I was twenty-seven years old when I finally had enough internal strength to say to myself, "I am still young and capable of creating a life much happier than this. I don't have to be miserable here forever." I left, and as painful as it was, I know I freed both myself and my ex-husband from a very unhappy life.

Suddenly, I was a single mom of three children, working full time while going to college. Despite my best efforts to foster self-worth, I was still plagued with insecurity. Being a divorced twenty-something with three children only heightened my belief that I was unlovable. I was overwhelmed with responsibility, pressure, self-doubt, and loneliness. I became severely depressed. My ex-husband found love quickly after our split, but I struggled considerably, latching on to unhealthy relationships and getting consumed by them.

Through this process, my poor Alex, who was already struggling with her parents' divorce—my ex-husband was her father in every way—also had to bear the burden of losing her mother to depression. I was irritable, distracted, short-tempered, and impatient. I asked a lot of her as the oldest sister. She was only in middle school, and I put too much responsibility on her. I was so consumed by my own unhappiness that I'm not sure I ever asked her how she was faring through the dissolve of her family. It makes me so sad and embarrassed to see that now.

I succumbed to a parenting mistake I see all too often in my practice today. I created a situation in which my child was worried about my well-being more than I was worried about hers. I was not wholly selfish or unfocused. I was channeling energy into making sure my kids had food and clothes, were getting their homework done, and were going to bed on time. I carted them to and from school and extracurricular activities. I went through the motions of parenting. However, I didn't attend to the emotional needs of my three girls. They were grappling with their parents' divorce and struggling to acclimate to an entirely new life. I didn't get it.

I didn't know how to give my daughters what they needed from me. I barely knew how to handle my own emotions. Alex, as an astute preteen, was a sponge soaking up the emotional energy I didn't realize I put out into our home. As I reflect, I recognize she probably knew I was depressed long before I did. She had to bear that burden alone, seeing that her mom was not okay, being totally ill-equipped for how to process it, and not being able to bring her fears or worries to me because I was the source of them.

Alex had to reconcile the divorce and the aftermath alone because I wasn't even clued in to what was happening to me or how it was hurting her. She needed a mother who recognized how much sadness, loss, anxiety, and uncertainty she felt after going through a divorce. She needed me to help her put words to her feelings, teach her how to soothe herself, and assure her that I was there for her every step of the way. She needed to know that whatever happened, she would be okay because I was there to guide and protect her. Instead, Alex got a mother who was drowning in her own loss and insecurity, who kept herself afloat, but who could not navigate her daughter through a terrible loss. I unwittingly set her adrift, and she feared for both herself and for me.

Ultimately, Alex's worry and fear morphed into anger and resentment. She struggled in school and began sneaking out at night and withdrawing from her sisters and me. She, too, became isolated and irritable. By that point, I had sought treatment for my depression and had stabilized considerably, but even when I saw the symptoms in my daughter, I perceived them as adolescent problem behaviors. I didn't recognize them as depression, and I certainly didn't see my role in creating her unhappiness.

We had several quarrelsome years together. Alex was angsty and rebellious, and I was exasperated and blaming. She became increasingly vocal and defiant as she got older. As she developed her voice and personal advocacy, she started using the word "abuse" to describe my mothering. I was horrified and dumbfounded. I knew abuse. I had survived it myself. I loved Alex. I had "done my best." I hadn't beaten her or physically abandoned her. I loved her as much as I could and tried to be a good mother even when I was hurting immeasurably. How could she use that painful word against me?

I tried to argue about it with her. We debated over semantics around what constitutes abuse and what doesn't. I gave her the old "You have it so much better than I did" song and dance. But somewhere deep down I knew I was so reactive to her accusations because I couldn't be 100 percent sure they didn't fit. I wanted to convince her that she was wrong so I wouldn't have to face the ways I had hurt her. When Alex told me how she was feeling, I expended a lot of energy trying to persuade her that her feelings were invalid. I regret that now. I wish I would have just held space for her and honored her experience as my daughter, even if I didn't agree with everything she said.

Ultimately, I realized that she was using the only language she had at the time to tell me she was experiencing trauma. I was not an abusive parent. But I was a hurting, wounded human who, despite my best intentions, had traumatized my child by way of my own trauma. Although this is a common occurrence, it brings up so much shame that people don't talk about it nearly enough. It was never normalized for me. My parents were dismissive and defensive about the ways they traumatized me. I had no model for how to make this right with Alex or manage my own shame. I felt alone, afraid, and, once again, ill-equipped to handle the challenge in front of me.

I finally came to a point where I realized I had to make a choice: hear my daughter or lose my relationship with her. I chose to listen. I'm so glad I did. I gave her something my parents never gave me. I acknowledged how difficult it was to live through the mistakes I made as a parent. I let her share her pain with me even though I was the one who caused it. I didn't ask her to protect me from the pain I caused her.

There was a reckoning. I honored Alex's experience. That felt both responsible and right but also really challenging. I gave her the gift of handing back to me the pain I placed on her. It wasn't her pain to carry. She deserved to hand it back. But it was heavy, and now I had to deal with my guilt. I fully believe there is no guilt in the world as agonizing as the guilt you feel as a parent.

While I was still in high school, I went to pack Alex's lunch one day and realized there was nothing suitable in the kitchen to give her. It must have been a while since my parents had been grocery shopping, and the best I could find was a Pop-Tart and a fruit cup to pack in her lunchbox. She went to a phenomenal preschool at Arizona State University where they grew fruits and vegetables in a garden, always had open art stations, and let the children run freely between the playground and classroom. It was quite progressive for the time, and here I was sending my kid to her fancy granola-mom preschool with a Pop-Tart for lunch.

I was sick with guilt. I felt terrible about it all day. I imagined all the other children opening their lunch boxes to healthy sandwiches and fresh-cut fruit and little notes from their moms while my poor, sweet Alex opened hers to find the stark, loveless silver packaging of a crappy Pop-Tart. I couldn't shake the guilt. It's been over twenty years, and I still think about that damn Pop-Tart. If I couldn't get over the Pop-Tart incident, how was I ever going to get over the fact that Alex felt I'd emotionally abandoned her after my divorce?

My parenting became driven by guilt. I wanted so badly to make amends that I stopped challenging her on anything. I practically gave in to her every demand. I was willing to do whatever I could to make it right for her, to ease her suffering. I became so clouded by guilt that I couldn't see how the tides had shifted. I was being manipulated. Not maliciously, but kids are both perceptive and opportunistic. Alex saw an opportunity to get her way with a few things, so she took it.

I was remarried by this time. Although I was blinded by guilt, the dynamic was clear to my husband. Finally, he intervened and helped me see I couldn't keep parenting from a place of guilt for the rest of my life. Doing that didn't honor Alex or me. I had to forgive myself and set up appropriate boundaries with her, so we could have the healthy mother-daughter relationship we both deserved.

I mustered up all my strength and had a heart-to-heart with her. The conversation went something like this: "I know I failed you in significant ways. You are so important to me, and I want to repair with you. I'm doing my best now to heal our relationship, but I can't be made to feel guilty about my mistakes forever. We can always process your feelings whenever you need to, but I cannot tolerate you bringing up the past every time you want something from me. I must live with myself. I need to like myself and sleep at night. I'm working to forgive myself, and I hope you can forgive me, too. I can never take back the years in which I failed you, but I promise to do right by you for the rest of my life if you'll let me." It was one of the hardest, bravest conversations I ever initiated.

There was initial pushback to be sure. People almost always push back when you set boundaries with them. But Alex, like most wounded children, wanted to forgive her mom. She didn't want the burden of anger and resentment hanging over her forever. She knew having a rift with me for the rest of her life wasn't healthy, and she knew I was a good, loving parent. She could see that through all my mistakes, I had never set out to hurt her. I was imperfect, as a woman, as a mother, and as a human. I owned my struggles and failures, and in doing so, I made a safe place for her to show up as a struggling, imperfect person as well. Through my vulnerability, I created a space where we could be imperfect humans together and have an honest, authentic relationship free of pretense or judgment.

The relationship that bloomed from that broken place is more amazing than I ever imagined. Alex is twenty-four years old as I write this, and I couldn't be happier with our connection. She calls me every time she has something to celebrate and every time she needs to cry with someone. She comes to me for advice, protection, and motherly wisdom. She seeks me out even when she doesn't want me to say a word but just needs a listener. By giving Alex the gift of my humility, vulnerability, and willingness, I opened the door to a deeply connected parent-child relationship.

It was all thanks to forgiveness: my desire to seek hers, to give it to myself, and to expect it from her once I had completed proper amends. To be clear, just saying "I'm sorry" wasn't enough. I created a living amends in which I showed her with my actions that I would show up for her the way she needed. I created a foundation of trust, and in my amends I earned my pardon. Alex and I both found great relief in forgiveness. Together we created a richly satisfying, wildly imperfect, wholehearted, loving relationship. In fact, ours is one of my all-time favorite love stories.

✦ ✦ ✦

At this point, you might be thinking about your relationship with your own parents. Perhaps you are questioning your relationship with your children. You may ask yourself, "Where have I traumatized my child along the way?" This is healthy. It's appropriate and even necessary to reflect on your behavior and make things right with the most important people in your life. It is healthy to question the people you love and ask them to make things right with you when warranted.

Healthy people permit themselves to feel discomfort and lean into it so they can move through the pain into healing. Anything else is just stuffing, ignoring, and distracting from the truth, which only results in heartache. So if you're feeling uncomfortable right now, good. Keep feeling it. Your discomfort holds a lesson about how to honor yourself and your closest relationships. Listen to your discomfort. It's your healthiest self calling.

## Dealing with Emotional Discomfort

I've found the best way to deal with the emotional discomfort that exists in relationships is to ask myself what I want in the end. What outcome does my heart seek? Initially, I wanted Alex to let me off the hook so I didn't have to face my guilt. But in my heart of hearts, I wanted a relationship with her. I wanted to be a good mother. I wanted to do the right thing, and I desperately wanted us to be close. When

I stripped away my fear and my ego, I was left with the raw truth of my heart's desire.

Once you are clear about your innermost needs, you can ask yourself what you need to do to achieve them. What will be most effective? Arguing with Alex's feelings was highly ineffective, but I found that being humble and letting her share her pain without being defensive was the path to our healing. You, too, can find self-forgiveness and relational healing when you seek out your heart's desire and are brave enough to do whatever it takes to meet your goal.

## Takeaways and Talking Points

+ Forgiveness is a gift you give yourself. Whether offering it to you or others, forgiveness allows you to put down the poison you've been drinking.

+ Self-forgiveness frees you from the shame and loathing that interferes with healthy connection.

+ When you hold compassion for yourself, you can validate the harm you've caused others from a healthy, grounded place. Only then can you honor and heal the relationship.

## Pack Your Self-Love Suitcase with Self-Forgiveness

It can be so hard to forgive ourselves when we've made terrible mistakes and hurt people we love. We often find it easier to forgive others than to forgive ourselves. Yet we are deserving of the same forgiveness we extend to those we love. Self-forgiveness begins with an acknowledgment that we are good people, even though we have done not-so-good things. When we can separate our innate goodness from our bad choices, we can extend forgiveness to ourselves and be empowered to make things right. When we fail to forgive ourselves, we stay powerless to improve our relationships with others and ourselves. To truly achieve self-love, we must learn to forgive ourselves.

## Chapter Six

# Letting Go of Toxic Relationships

*You will evolve past certain people.*
*Let yourself.*

— Mandy Hale

Alex and I were lucky. We were able to repair our relationship in a healthy way. Unfortunately, it isn't always possible to rebuild and move forward in a relationship. Sometimes the most self-loving choice you can make is to walk away from a toxic person or a toxic relationship even when it is the last thing you want to do. I have one more case example for you before I start putting together the action steps for becoming a self-loving person. This is the story of Esther and her challenge to love herself enough to walk away from a harmful relationship.

◆ ◆ ◆

# The Story of Esther

"Esther" met her husband, "Dominic," at work. He was a successful dentist, and she was his office manager. He was married when he hired her but often complained about his ungrateful and unaffectionate wife. Dominic groomed Esther by trying to elicit her sympathy. He portrayed himself as a devoted, hardworking husband and father who did everything in his power to live up to his selfish and demanding wife's high expectations.

Esther and Dominic worked long hours together and were often the last two people in the office each evening. He lamented about how his wife stayed home all day, spent his money, and treated him like an ATM. Esther believed every word. She began to envy Dominic's wife and her "easy" lifestyle. She imagined how appreciative and happy she would be if she were his wife. She told herself she would love him the way he deserved.

Their affair began at the office and was full of passion. They filled each other with all the words each of them longed to hear. Dominic told Esther how beautiful, kind, and amazing she was. He told her how he wished he had met her first, and he weaved together stories of the places they would travel and the life they would have together "if only." In turn, Esther stroked Dominic's ego in every way she could. She listened to him vent about his wife and validated how terrible she was to him. She told him how brilliant and tolerant he was. She spoke of how much more he deserved and how doting she would be if she were his wife. Over time, her desire to win his heart grew stronger and stronger.

Esther was an intelligent, kind person. She never saw herself as a "homewrecker." She did not want to break up a family. She allowed herself to be swayed by the stories Dominic fed her about his "miserable wife" and his "loveless marriage." She wanted so badly to be loved by him. She convinced herself it would be in everyone's best interest, even his children's, if Dominic left his wife. She never thought to herself, "I don't care if the children are damaged, I'm going to get what I want." That wasn't in her nature. Instead, she said to herself, "His children need to see a loving relationship. We can model a healthy marriage for them."

## Cognitive Dissonance

Esther fell victim to cognitive dissonance, a psychological state in which one's values compete with their behavior. Cognitive dissonance is defined as "the state of having inconsistent thoughts, beliefs, or attitudes, especially as relating to behavioral decisions and attitude change." Behaving in a way that is inconsistent with your values is painful. When this happens, the brain looks for a way to rationalize the behavior to reinstate internal harmony. Because Esther was a kind person who did not want to hurt others, her brain looked for ways to trick herself into thinking the affair was somehow a good thing for the people she was hurting.

Dominic likely experienced his own cognitive dissonance. He was at an impasse with his wife. He did not know how to engage with her differently or create his own happiness. He rationalized that his needs were not being met in his marriage. Because he lacked self-awareness around the ways he contributed to the marital dysfunction, he felt entitled to have an affair. Cognitive dissonance is sneaky that way. It's a common phenomenon, but it requires acute self-awareness to know you're experiencing it.

Ultimately, Esther got her wish. Dominic's wife discovered the affair and threw him out of the house. He moved in with Esther, and she supported him through a painful divorce. She remained steadfast in her love for him even as he became filled with regret and tried to repair things with his wife. She stayed by his side when his wife refused him and initiated a contentious child custody battle. She knew there would be a difficult transition period, but never in her fantasies had Esther imagined the chaos and distress that became her reality.

Esther got pregnant during the divorce proceedings, and she and Dominic were married soon after his divorce was final. Their wedding was clouded by the anger his two teenage sons had toward them because of the affair. The boys never accepted Esther into their lives and always saw her as the woman who broke their mother's heart and destroyed their family.

Esther did her best to create a loving home despite the agonizing conflict. About two years after her daughter was born, she discovered Dominic was having an affair with one of his patients. The patient called her at home to expose the relationship and threatened to file a lawsuit against Dominic. They quickly entered therapy as a couple where Dominic disclosed he had a long history of infidelities, both in his first marriage and with her.

Dominic expressed remorse and recognized he had a significant problem. He committed to exploring the origins of his out-of-control behavior and vowed to become the husband Esther deserved. Despite her anger and heartbreak, Esther did not want to get divorced. She loved Dominic and wanted to keep her family together. She made the commitment to stay in the marriage if Dominic could get and stay healthy. They developed a solid relationship recovery plan that included transparency, accountability, and boundaries. Esther was hopeful.

Despite Dominic's early commitment and Esther's willingness, the relationship continued to deteriorate. Esther expressed frustration that Dominic was agitated and resentful about the accountability plan they instituted. Even though they agreed Esther could look at his phone and email for a time to create renewed trust and transparency, he became angry each time she did.

Dominic was unable to stay in a place of empathy and understanding when Esther became angry, suspicious, jealous, or hurt. He could not make space for her when she was tearful and hopeless. He wanted her to "move forward" and "stop living in the past." He accused her of "just trying to punish him" and being unwilling to heal and move on.

Esther and Dominic stayed in therapy for a considerable amount of time but made little progress. While Dominic presented as arrogant, impatient, and selfish, deep down he hid an enormous amount of shame. It was so painful to look at how destructive he had been to so many people who loved him that he couldn't bring himself to do the vulnerable work needed to recover. Instead, he stayed in a childish, demanding state, asking Esther to subdue her intense emotions so as not to elicit the shame and guilt he found unbearable.

Time and again, he responded to Esther's pain with irritation and continued to justify his hurtful minimization of her feelings. It's quite common for someone to act out of anger, to appear selfish and even narcissistic when they feel inadequate at their core. This is an unconscious self-preservation technique that serves to keep one from crumbling into hating oneself. However, Dominic's unwillingness to shift out of his unhealthy defense mechanisms was destroying his marriage.

The final blow came when Esther discovered an email account Dominic had created to communicate with women without her knowledge. The exchanges she found were flirtatious in nature but did not provide evidence he had had another physical affair. Dominic maintained that he never cheated again but felt so trapped by Esther's "constant hovering, anger, and accusations" that he "needed an escape." Basically, he blamed her for his repeated betrayals.

Esther decided she could not tolerate it anymore. She had done everything in her power to save the marriage. She did her best to understand her husband and recognize his behaviors were about his own deep-seated insecurities. She gave him time to figure out his heart and become the man he said he wanted to be.

Through everything, Esther became stronger and healthier. She clarified her values and knew how to live within them. She understood the self-esteem issues that made her vulnerable to the advances of a married man. She resolved to take better care of herself. Esther could see her worth and advocate for herself, but she could not make her husband meet her needs. When she realized he was not willing to do the work to be the husband she needed, she had to make a painful decision. Esther had two choices: accept that she could not change her husband and live in the marriage as it was or leave and create a life in which her needs would be met.

Esther's heart was heavy when she filed for divorce. She loved Dominic and wanted to stay married. In many ways, her heart told her to stay. But Esther had come to a place where she loved herself too much to tolerate disrespectful, unloving behavior from her partner any longer. She did not see Dominic as a monster. Even though he had wounded her terribly, she was able to see his behavior as a sign of his own brokenness. She worked on her emotional health and gave him space to heal, too, but ultimately, he wasn't willing to make the journey.

## Tolerating Unhealthy Behaviors

The sad truth is some people will choose to stay unhealthy. You will never be able to force another person into wellness. Becoming the best version of yourself is painful work that insists you delve into the darkest parts of yourself. It requires an enormous amount of courage to be so vulnerable, and not everyone is willing to do it. Many will decide it is more comfortable to stay unhealthy, to ignore the ugly parts of them, and to just keep doing what is familiar and safe. Not everyone aspires to be their best self. You must honor that, but it doesn't mean you have to tolerate it in your life.

An essential lesson on the path to self-love is you cannot honor yourself thoroughly when you allow others in your life to dishonor you. We must be willing to see all people as imperfect and make a space for mistakes, forgiveness, and repair. However, we must also recognize when a person is incapable of meeting our needs. Whether it is with a parent, romantic partner, employer, or friend, when a relationship creates more pain than satisfaction, we must be willing to evaluate the role that relationship plays in our life.

A self-loving person will ask themselves, "How is this relationship good for me? Why am I staying? What is my motivation to be here?" If the answer sounds anything like, "Well, he's my dad, I'm obligated to care for him ... I'm staying for the kids ... I'm afraid to be alone ... I'd be mortified to tell people what was really going on," or "She is always so sorry after she acts like that," it is time to reevaluate. Self-loving people do not stay in harmful relationships. They do not see guilt or fear as a reason to tolerate toxic behavior from others.

Let me be perfectly clear. Outside of parenting your young or adolescent children, you are under no obligation to stay in any kind of relationship with anyone. You don't owe anybody anything. You deserve to be healthy. You deserve to be in healthy relationships with healthy people. Anyone who consistently disappoints, hurts, betrays, demeans, judges, or takes advantage of you does not belong in your life. No matter who they are, no matter what good things they might have brought to your life in the past, no matter how sorry you feel for them because of their own trauma, no matter how great they are "sometimes," you are under no obligation to stay in a relationship that makes you feel rejected, unloved, devalued, or insignificant. You are too valuable for that nonsense.

One thing I have heard from clients time and again is, "I don't know why I attract unhealthy people." Let's set the record straight. You attract people who are about as healthy as you are. Healthy people attract other healthy people. Unhealthy people attract other unhealthy people. Healthy people are not drawn to unhealthy people and will not tolerate relationships with unhealthy people. If all or most of your relationships are unhealthy, you are the common denominator. Ouch. I know. Stay with me, though.

If that's the bad news, here is the good news. You have the power to shift out of being an unhealthy person who tolerates unhealthy relationships. You can choose happiness. You can choose to love and respect yourself. Quite frankly, you are too smart, too worthy, and too much of a miracle to waste one more day treating yourself like crap and allowing others to do the same.

So here is my challenge to you. If you determine you are in an unhealthy relationship, look at yourself and how you contribute to the dysfunction. Make the necessary changes to show up as your best, healthiest self, and see what shifts you can create in the relationship. This way, if you do decide to leave, you can do so with more peace of mind, knowing you gave the relationship every opportunity to be different. Plus, you decrease the chances of leaving one dysfunctional relationship just to enter into another, or starting a new relationship as your best self and then wondering if things could have been different in the first relationship had you shown up in a healthier way.

## Takeaways and Talking Points

+ Unhealthy people attract unhealthy relationships. You have the power to become a healthier person and change the relationships in your life.

+ Do the necessary work to become your best self and give your dysfunctional relationships an opportunity to transform and heal.

+ Know that as you grow into a better version of yourself, you may find some relationships don't make sense for you anymore. You don't have to tolerate toxic relationships for any reason. You have the right to expect people in your life to treat you with respect.

+ You also must honor that some people won't be willing to change the way they treat you. You can't force anyone else to change.

+ If someone isn't willing to honor you, you must decide what you need to do to honor yourself.

## Pack Your Self-Love Suitcase
## with Self-Respect

You are almost fully packed, but there is one more item to add to your skillset before you begin traversing the path to self-love. Self-respect is essential for self-love because people who love themselves don't allow others to treat them badly. Self-loving people use healthy assertiveness to let others know where they stand, set appropriate boundaries, and stand up for themselves. Because it can be so difficult to be assertive when the concept is new to you, try asking yourself, "If I loved myself, would I put up with this? What would a self-loving person do in my position?" Sometimes behaving as if you love yourself can be a great first step in becoming more self-loving.

# Part Two:

# YOUR INNER WARRIOR UNLEASHED

# Chapter Seven

# Transform Understanding into Action

*Your greatest self has been*
*waiting your whole life;*
*don't make it wait any longer.*

—Steve Maraboli

In Part Two of this book, we're going to shift from learning why you don't love yourself to determining how to forge a path toward self-love. Here's where you figure out how to be the person you're truly meant to be (and who you already are buried beneath the garbage that weighs you down). Since I've already provided so much information about the origins of self-loathing, I think it's helpful to recap what I've written so far to be sure you understand how to apply the knowledge to your own life.

To be clear, you cannot move into the action phase of this book before you really appreciate your own history and how your past set you up to not love yourself. You must connect to the child you once were and see the innate goodness and worthiness inside that young person. You must develop a desire to love, protect, and grow that person into the most authentic version of yourself.

Your original self and your best adult self are forever connected. You can't love one without the other, and you can't be one without the other. Without this foundational connection, all the action steps I present moving forward will feel hollow. You can try them, and you may have minimal success, but hear this: You won't be able to fully connect to the work and become your best self if you don't believe you are innately worthy of getting there. It is probably easiest to conceptualize the path to self-love in steps. I've created seven steps and will present them throughout the next several chapters. As much as I'd love to tell you that you can do seven quick and easy steps to achieve self-love, it's not that simple. Each step in my book is a stage of self-discovery. I will present concepts and theories that will aid in your self-discovery process. Also, I'll provide exercises for understanding the concepts and putting the ideas into actions that will improve your life. Ready? Let's do this.

## Step One:
## Evaluate Your Internal Voice

In Step One, you will evaluate your internal dialogue to determine your negative core beliefs. These beliefs dictate the way you speak to yourself. If you find yourself saying things like, "You're such an idiot! That was so stupid. You can't do anything right," your core belief is probably something like, "I am not good enough, I am stupid, I am defective, I am worthless, I am not lovable," or something similar.

Some people can identify their negative self-talk and their core beliefs easily. For others, it is such a deeply rooted part of their existence that they don't notice it at all. I have had clients who were shocked to learn not everybody has an "itty bitty shitty committee" inside their head telling them what a loser they are. "Isn't that normal?" they ask. Well, it's not uncommon, but if you define "normal" as healthy or appropriate or helpful, then no. Nature never intended for you to flog yourself with criticism. A negative inner voice is unhealthy, and you've got to get control over it. You might not eliminate it entirely, but you don't have to be hostage to it any longer. You must recognize it for what it is, reject it completely, and reframe your thoughts in a self-loving way.

## EXERCISE: IDENTIFY YOUR NEGATIVE SELF-TALK

If you need help identifying your negative self-talk, put a few reminders on your phone throughout the day. When a reminder pops up, ask yourself, "How have I spoken to myself in the last few hours?" Specifically, what statements have you made to yourself about yourself? Be specific and write them down. If you were in a business meeting, you might have said to yourself, "I have a great idea that could really solve this problem," or "This problem is really tricky. I'm not sure what to do yet." Perhaps you said something like, "Oh my god, what am I doing here? I have nothing to contribute, and I'm way out of my league. Any day now they are all going to figure out what an idiot I am, and I'm going to get fired."

If your self-talk is more like the latter, make a log of these self-defeating statements. Keep a pad of paper, a notebook, a day planner, anything you can use as a journal. You can also keep digital notes if that is easier. You might want to go ahead and do it right now.

Seriously. Doing this exercise is a critical first step in the process. Please don't read all these steps and think about each action item for a moment without ever doing the exercises. Self-love isn't going to emerge from simply reading the words on these pages. You must seek it out with action.

Did you do it yet? If not, bookmark this page and come back with your journal in tow.

With this exercise, I usually see one of two reactions. Some people see how unreasonable and untrue their internal voices can be. Other people will look at a long list of self-deprecating remarks and say, "Yup. This is me. I'm a total loser." If you're in that second group, don't despair. You are not the loser you tell yourself you are, and you are fully capable of being the happy, confident, and self-loving person you long to be. It might take a little more effort, but you are fully capable of getting there.

Once you have a compilation of the negative self-talk you engage in, you need to connect it to the negative core beliefs you hold about yourself. Dr. Aaron Beck, the developer of cognitive theory describes negative core beliefs as distorted thoughts people develop because of adverse early life experiences. These distorted thoughts create a "cognitive triad" in which people form a negative view of themselves, the world, and the future. This framework becomes a lens through which they see everything in their world, and it can taint and distort their life experience.

## Validating and Reinforcing Core Beliefs

For example, if I have a negative core belief that I am unlovable, I will see it as directly correlated to my inability to be loved when a person in my life hurts, disappoints, or rejects me. Whatever our beliefs, we find ways to validate them and reinforce them. This means I won't consider that the problem might be with the other person, and I won't expect or insist people treat me better. I will accept all kinds of unacceptable behavior from others because I think my unworthiness is the reason people mistreat me. I don't feel worthy of love, kindness, and respect, so I will accept virtually any kind of behavior from others because I am just happy to have people in my life at all.

When others mistreat me, I will see it as evidence that I am unlovable. This belief will be reinforced every time I am treated poorly by others. I will be trapped in a vicious cycle wherein I am mistreated by others over and over because I expect it, I accept it, and my belief system is attracting people who will exploit my insecurity and self-doubt. The truth is, we teach people how to treat us based on what we will tolerate and what we won't.

Generally, negative core beliefs fall into a few broad categories: defectiveness, unlovability, safety, powerlessness, and responsibility. Let's look at these a little more closely and break them down. You may want to highlight the negative beliefs that resonate most for you.

### *Defectiveness*

Those who have a defective core belief might think, "I am worthless; I am not good enough; I am stupid; I am ugly; I am bad; I am a failure," or "There is something wrong with me." People who see themselves as defective have endured repeated life experiences that reinforce their lack of capability. They may have been the baby in a large family of successful older siblings, or they may have had difficulties learning or have a naturally shy temperament. As adults, they may avoid conflict or be afraid to make decisions. They may lean on others to help them navigate through life or avoid doing anything they aren't confident they can do well.

## Unlovability

Those with a core belief of being unlovable might think, "I am alone," "I am unwanted," "I will always be rejected," "I don't matter," "My needs aren't important," or "I don't deserve love." These are the people who were rejected by peers and bullied in school. They may have had neglectful or emotionally unavailable caregivers. They grew up chronically receiving a message that they weren't accepted, valued, or important to others. As adults, they may be needy and clingy in relationships or be overly self-protective and avoidant of emotional intimacy.

## Safety

A negative core belief around safety sounds like "I'm not safe," "People will hurt me," "I can't take care of myself," and "I'm in danger." This core belief is often associated with significant trauma. There may have been chronic abuse or neglect. Perhaps there was a lack of basic needs like food and shelter. A powerful single-incident trauma can cause this core belief, like the death of a parent or a terrible car accident that resulted in permanent injury. Ultimately, people who feel unsafe are fearful, anxious, and agitated adults. They are chronic worriers, and others may experience them as taking the fun out of any situation.

## Powerlessness

The powerless category of negative self-talk sounds like "I'm weak," "I'm helpless," "I am out of control," "I need to be in control," and "I'm trapped." This is another core belief that can manifest from abuse or neglect. As adults, these individuals may present as apathetic, resigning themselves to whatever life hands them. "Well, there's nothing I can do about it" might be their response to even small challenges. Without intervention, these people may fail to live up to their potential despite how creative, smart, or talented they are because they lack courage when faced with adversity.

### *Responsibility*

Finally, those with a responsibility core belief tell themselves, "It's my fault," "I have to do this alone," "It's not okay to ask for help," "I can't trust anyone," and "I have to be perfect." Critical, perfectionistic, and demanding caregivers can instill this negative belief. If you grew up constantly hearing "You should have known better," or "You're the older sibling, you need to set an example," you might be an adult with a responsibility complex. These people are highly functional as adults. They often have very successful careers and rarely ask for help. They may have difficulty admitting when they are wrong and be defensive when questioned. Their self-image is built on the belief they must be perfect, or right, or know how to do everything. As you might imagine, this is utterly exhausting for them and those close to them.

Now ask yourself, "Which negative core beliefs do I hold about myself?" You might identify with several, and that's okay. If you feel overwhelmed by the sheer number of negative core beliefs you hold, don't panic. I'm going to help guide you through the process of changing them. Once you know what your negative self-talk sounds like and what core beliefs are driving it, you are ready for Step Two.

## Takeaways and Talking Points

✦ Identify your negative self-talk by checking in with yourself at regular intervals and documenting your self-statements in a journal.

✦ The most common negative core beliefs (defectiveness, unlovability, safety, powerlessness, and responsibility) directly correlate to your negative self-talk. Identify those most applicable to you.

# Chapter Eight

# Releasing Trauma

*The knowledge of the past stays with us.*
*To let go is to release the images and*
*emotions, the grudges and fears,*
*the clingings and disappointments of*
*the past that bind our spirit.*

—Jack Kornfield

S tep Two on the path to self-love requires that you determine
where your faulty belief system developed. Remember, humans
are born with the innate capacity and desire to love themselves. Children living in healthy environments are confident and often proud of
themselves. We all come into the world like this. It is only through
negative life experiences that our self-loving proclivities are stripped
away from us.

The best example of this comes from a groundbreaking research
project conducted in Southern California through the Centers for
Disease Control and Prevention (CDC) and Kaiser Permanente in the
late 1990s. The Adverse Childhood Experience (ACE) Study included
over 17,000 participants who provided personal information used to

link adverse childhood experiences to mental and physical health problems in adulthood. Participants completed a survey that offered them an ACE score. The results were staggering.

There was a direct correlation between the number of ACEs a person had and their physical and mental health in adulthood. The survey consisted of ten questions that fell into three different categories: abuse, neglect, and household dysfunction. This last one is important because it shows you don't have to be a victim of child abuse to experience long-standing wellness issues that are directly correlated to your early home life. Of the ten questions, three ask about abuse—physical, emotional, and sexual. Two ask about neglect—physical and emotional. The other five ask about household dysfunction—if your parents ever divorced or separated, if either of your parents had a mental illness or substance abuse problem, if you had a family member who was incarcerated, or if there was violence between the adults in your home.

Not only did the ACE study show that the more adverse childhood experiences a person has the more significant their risk for physical and mental health issues in adulthood, but it also revealed that the presence of even one ACE is enough to change a person's long-term health outcomes. This means that even if you had a relatively happy childhood, if your parents fought all the time or were divorced, or if one of your parents drank too much, you've got an ACE. Even one ACE likely changed your belief system about yourself and the world, and ultimately, it may have changed the trajectory of your life.

I don't mean to send a message of doom and gloom here. I have an ACE score of five, which is pretty hard core and basically means I have significant risk for a whole host of ailments, including depression, anxiety, alcoholism and drug addiction, teen pregnancy, suicide, cancer, liver disease, STDs, domestic violence, obesity, stroke, heart disease, becoming a rape victim, and more. So that sucks. As you already know, I have experienced some of these conditions—*Why, hello there, depression and teen pregnancy.* But the good news is I've made peace with my childhood, am in good physical health, and enjoy emotional health as well. I love myself; I'm a productive, well-educated member of society; and I have healthy relationships with all the most important people in my life.

## Step Two:
## Unpack Your Personal Trauma History

The moral of the story is that no matter what your ACE score, you are not a hopeless case. You may have more challenges to overcome than a person with a lower score, but you are still fully capable of having a beautiful life and a happy, peaceful heart. If you are interested in finding out your ACE score, you can flip to the back of the book to take the survey.

The other moral of the story I'm telling is, just because you didn't have a wildly traumatic childhood doesn't mean your childhood didn't affect you in profound and unhealthy ways. Sometimes one of my biggest jobs as a psychologist is helping a client understand why they are struggling. People can be so quick to dismiss their early life experiences and blame all their current problems on their own innate defectiveness. While not uncommon, it is so unhelpful to blindly protect and defend the people who raised you while blaming yourself for everything. It doesn't need to be a blame game.

## The Power of Meaningful Change

All I want you to do is acknowledge that your life experiences impacted the adult you have become. When you do that, you give yourself the power to make meaningful changes. Otherwise, you risk falling into a trap of believing something is inherently wrong with you and that you're powerless to fix it. When we view our struggles as the result of our experiences, we recognize that most of our unhelpful traits are learned and can be unlearned, thus reclaiming our power and ability to change ourselves and our circumstances.

Look, parents are people. People are imperfect. We have weaknesses. We make mistakes. Good, loving parents do unhelpful things in their parenting that hurt their kids and distort their self-image and worldview. It's incredibly common, and it doesn't mean your parents were bad people or bad parents. It doesn't mean you have to be angry at them forever, confront them, or cut them out of your life. It just means the people who raised you were human. Their human shortcomings impacted you. Your human shortcomings affect the people in your life, too. It's totally normal and not something to be ashamed of. It's the human experience. We are all in this together.

## The Trauma Egg

The reason Step Two requires deep reflection into your history is so you can understand both who your original self is and how your original self was distorted by your unique life experiences. At my practice, we use a method developed by Marilyn Murray to help clients explore their pasts and make connections from their early life experiences to their current struggles. She calls this technique the Trauma Egg. It's basically an inventory of all a person's adverse childhood experiences. While the ACE study defined adverse childhood experiences in limitation, on the Trauma Egg we include all painful life experiences. We cover specific events such as getting bullied at school, being involved in a car accident, or dealing with the death of a grandparent, and subtler, pervasive experiences like extreme poverty, a parent's rage issues, impossibly high expectations, and the like.

I tell my clients, "If it left a negative impact on you, it's trauma, and it belongs on the egg." Many struggle with whether an ordeal was "big enough" to warrant inclusion on their timeline. Using self-compassion as our guiding principle, we recognize that any painful circumstance is important and worthy of honoring no matter how insignificant we tell ourselves it was in retrospect. Others say, "Yes, but isn't that just life? Bad things happen to everyone!" Well yes, that's true, and each of those bad things shapes us. Just because bad things happen to everyone doesn't mean we aren't allowed to have feelings about the ones that happen to us. Hurt and pain are part of the human experience. They're part of what connects us to other people, so honoring them allows us to empathize and identify with others. Minimizing the feelings makes us dismissive and isolates us from others.

### Are My Feelings Valid?

Sometimes the next comment is, "But what about people with terrible childhoods? There are kids out there who are being seriously abused or are homeless and starving. My childhood wasn't that bad. I can't complain." Reality check: Life isn't a contest in which only the person with the worst childhood in the history of the world is allowed to have feelings about their early life experiences. You don't have to earn your right to have emotions. If something made you sad or embarrassed, or sent you the message that you were unworthy or unimportant, then it mattered. You get to have feelings about it.

Telling yourself (or anyone else) that they "shouldn't" feel the way they feel is about the most unhelpful approach out there. You feel what you feel. Emotions aren't "right" or "wrong"; they just are. You can tell yourself, "Sure I was bullied by Joey as a kid, but I didn't know what he was going through. It turns out his dad was an alcoholic and was beating him, so it makes sense that he was a bully. I shouldn't have taken it so personally." It may be helpful to your healing process to practice empathy for someone who harmed you, but using that empathy to undermine your experience is not beneficial. It really doesn't matter to the eight-year-old version of you that Joey had a difficult home life. Seeing that in retrospect will not change the painful emotions you experienced at the time or shift the negative messages about yourself that you internalized and carried with you from the experience.

It is much more healing to recognize how painful it was, honor the pain with loving-kindness, and empathize for that younger version of you. Validate the messages you internalized as a child. They may not have been true, but they felt real at the time. "Yes, it makes sense that I told myself I was unlikable when Joey bullied me. That was so painful. Poor, sweet, little me. I was likable, but it was hard to see that when I was being treated so terribly by a peer. I have been carrying that ugly message with me ever since. I can see now that the message I internalized was not a true message but rather a message handed to me from a difficult life experience."

When you can reframe your experience in that way, you are using your adult wisdom to prepare yourself to let go of that old, untrue message and replace it with a healthier, more realistic one. Indeed, coupling that compassion for yourself with compassion for those who have injured you is helpful and engages the wisest part of you. Just don't skip over the self-compassion part.

## EXERCISE: TAKE YOUR TRAUMA INVENTORY

While there are many ways to write a trauma history, Marilyn's Trauma Egg involves drawing a large oval on a large piece of paper. The oval is the "egg," which is a metaphor for you. You are the egg. Your traumas are the cracks in your egg or, more literally, the cracks in your self-concept and worldview.

As a therapist walks a client through their Trauma Egg, they help you define your traumas (the events), and then break down the meaning you attached to your experience. Therapists do this by identifying what happened, what emotions were felt, what messages were taken in about you or the world, how you coped with it, and what you needed that you didn't get.

Using this model to help you connect all of your difficult early life experiences produces an objective, visual compilation of the themes that emerged from your journey. These themes created the negative core beliefs identified in Step One. Laying it all out on paper can produce an understanding of how you came to see yourself and the world the way you do. It also helps identify how you developed unhealthy coping skills and how those coping skills were reinforced over time.

# TRAUMA EGG

For each event inside
the egg, include:

✦ Age *(How old were you?)*

✦ Event
*(Describe briefly what happened.)*

✦ Emotions
*(How did you feel?/What did you need to feel?)*

✦ Messages
*(What did you make up or believe about yourself?)*

✦ Coping *(How did you cope?)*

✦ Needed *(What did you need or deserve?)*

9-years old—Parents divorced; lots of fighting; don't know
where I will live. Scared, confused, angry. I cannot trust
others; I have to take care of myself. Coped by watching TV,
hiding in room. Needed explanations, comfort, and security.

8-years old—Broke my leg and in the hospital for a month;
parents not allowed to visit me. Scared, alone, abandoned.
I'm alone. Stuffed emotions, watched TV.
Needed comfort, nurturing, and reassurance.

7-years old—My dog was killed by a car. Sad.
I should get over it. Coped by stuffing my sadness,
avoided it. Needed to grieve.

### Illustration of the Trauma Egg

Let's return to the bullying example. Here's how that might look on the Trauma Egg.

+ *Age and Event*: Joey bullied me from fourth through sixth grade. He threw rubber bands and erasers at me on the bus, tripped me when I walked by, and called me names like "fatty four eyes."
+ *Emotion*: Hurt, shame, loneliness, and rejection.
+ *Messages*: I am not likable. I am fat. I am ugly. There is something wrong with me.
+ *Coping*: Isolation. I tried to be invisible. I never spoke up in class. I sat at the back of the room and the back of the bus. I avoided doing anything I thought might bring attention to me. I cried alone in my room.
+ *Needed*: I needed the bus driver and my teachers to notice and intervene. I needed an adult to tell me I was valuable and put a stop to the bullying.

I love watching the light bulbs go off as clients put together their Trauma Egg. Suddenly, they can say, "It wasn't all my fault. It makes sense that I'm like this!" We use this tool to shift a person's questioning from "What's wrong with me" to "What happened to me?" Once a person can see their struggles and "weaknesses" as a direct result of their life experiences rather than innate defectiveness, self-compassion begins to take hold. Self-compassion is the train we must board to arrive back at our original self, or "original child," as Marilyn coined it.

When making your Trauma Egg remember that not all traumas are specific events. Make sure to include all painful life experiences, especially those that were subtle and pervasive. If you had a parent with a drinking problem but they weren't abusive, you might think you weren't affected by it. More likely, your parent was emotionally unavailable due to chronic intoxication, and you may have missed out on important emotional attunement and meaningful connection. Such a situation would negatively impact the way you see yourself and how you inter-act in relationships, so it's worth including on your Trauma Egg. Other examples of chronic, painful experiences might be having a parent who was a workaholic, having a sibling who was highly favored by a parent, having learning difficulties, or being criticized for your looks or abilities.

## *A Word of Warning*

This feels like the time to say the thing many readers might not want to hear. Not everyone is going to be able to read a self-help book (or even twenty self-help books) and come to a place of emotional wellness on their own. If you are a survivor of significant trauma or abuse, it is unlikely you will get where you want to be without the guidance and support of a skilled therapist. There is no shame in this. My personal wellness is a product of a lot of great therapists whom I have so much gratitude toward. I would not have wanted to make my Trauma Egg alone. I needed the support of a therapist who could walk that painful road with me, help me process and make sense of things along the way, give me tools for managing the painful emotions that came up as I did the work, and make me feel cared for, validated, and connected to someone through it all.

Think of it this way: If you were diagnosed with a potentially fatal disease, would you decide to treat it yourself with the guidance of a self-help book on clean eating and healing meditation? Probably not. More likely, you would recognize the seriousness of the situation and seek the counsel of a medical professional specializing in the treatment of that disease. Trauma shares some similarities, in that healing from it correctly often requires employing the wisdom and guidance of a specialized healthcare professional, aka a highly skilled trauma therapist.

Step Two may require getting a therapist. Maybe it won't. You'll have to decide for yourself if your trauma history is one you feel capable of unpacking on your own. If you get started and find you are getting emotionally overwhelmed, stuck, or are unable to connect to the experiences or see how they contribute to your current struggles, you probably need a therapist to walk you through the process.

## EXERCISE: CONNECT WITH YOUR INNER CHILD

Once you have developed an understanding of where your negative core beliefs came from, you need to connect with who you were before all that garbage started dulling your shine. I'm talking again about relating to your original self. As I discussed earlier, the stuffed animal assignment is a great way to get connected to the original version of you. Make a representation of your young self to capture the essence of your authentic self and to have a tangible reminder to look at every day. Other activities for making this connection include art projects. For example,

+ Draw a picture of yourself at different ages to capture not only who you were originally, but how your life experiences shifted who you became over time.
+ Write a letter to your young self offering love, support, wisdom, explanation, and encouragement.
+ Write a letter from your young self to your adult self. Let the child in you tell your adult self what they need from you today to feel safe, secure, loved, and important.

That kid has been through enough. When you don't love and honor yourself, when you criticize and degrade yourself, when you let people mistreat you, and when you hold yourself back from chasing after your wildest dreams, you perpetuate the trauma that child experienced. It's time to cut that crap out right now. Give that precious child the life they deserve. You are not responsible for everything that happened to you when you were young. But as an adult, you are responsible for cleaning up your own life, for loving and respecting yourself, and for making sure you don't keep hurting that little kid inside you (or the adult, for that matter). Once you are committed to that work, you are ready for Step Three.

## Takeaways and Talking Points

+ You've done the difficult work of unpacking your personal trauma story by completing a trauma inventory. This exercise helped you identify the origins of your negative core beliefs, which guide your critical self-talk.

+ Now that you understand where these untrue beliefs came from, you can begin connecting to your inner child, the one who was wounded long ago and needs the love and care of your adult self. Connecting to your inner child will prepare you for the work of rebuilding your self-worth.

# CHAPTER NINE

# Yes, You Deserve Happiness

*Your task is not to seek for love, but
merely to seek and find all the barriers
within yourself that you have
built against it.*

—Rumi

Step Three will look a little different for everyone. For me, Step Three was forgiving myself and letting go of toxic relationships. Once I cleaned house, so to speak, I made space to do the work of empowering and loving myself fully. In my work with clients, I have seen many who needed to start practicing love and empowerment before they were ready to forgive themselves or walk away from toxic relationships. Once you have set up the foundation for self-love, you begin to rebuild your sense of self-worth, which is a profoundly personal experience. Give yourself permission to do it in a way that feels safe and most productive for you.

## Step Three: Build Your Self-Worth

In this step, evaluate what holds you back from feeling worthy of the life you desire. My unworthy beliefs came from childhood. I received direct messages of unworthiness from both of my stepparents, and although my parents showed me love in many ways, their lack of protection confirmed my stepparents' overt messaging. The pain I felt manifested into unhealthy coping mechanisms that carried into adulthood. Ultimately, my sense of unworthiness and my inadequate coping contributed to poor decisions I made that hurt people I loved. Then my guilt and shame caused me to feel unworthy of any happiness at all. As a result, I tolerated unhealthy relationships, let people mistreat me, and treated myself poorly. Each stage of my life laid a foundation for the next and made me more and more vulnerable to a poor self-image and to my mental health symptoms. That's how this vicious cycle of self-loathing develops.

Consider the examples presented in earlier chapters. "Maria" felt unworthy because she wasn't perfect. "Nyah" felt unworthy because her parents abandoned her. "Ling" felt unworthy because she had dyslexia. Ask yourself now, "What were the painful experiences of my life that led me to feel unworthy of attaining my heart's desire?"

The work of Step Three is to reject the notion that you are not worthy of the life you desire. Self-compassion is a crucial element of this step. Making a Trauma Egg will almost certainly bring up feelings of self-compassion. Once I felt compassion for the sixteen-year-old who struggled to take care of herself and her daughter, I softened toward myself. I saw myself as flawed but doing my best. When I looked back even further in my inventory, I felt compassion for the girl who was vulnerable to depression and teen pregnancy because of childhood trauma.

Through the lens of self-compassion, I saw myself not as unworthy but as wounded. My compassionate adult self longed to heal the wounds of the young girl I once was. I started believing I was worthy of happiness. Feeling worthy allowed me to take the next necessary steps, which for me meant forgiving myself and making amends to my daughter. At that point, the path was clear for me to begin loving myself and pursuing my dreams.

## EXERCISE: ENGAGE IN SELF-COMPASSION PRACTICES

What makes you feel unworthy of your heart's desire? How can you exercise compassion for the person who developed that sense of unworthiness? What action steps can you take to open yourself up to self-love? It might be helpful to write this out. When you catch that harsh voice in your head trying to talk you out of self-compassion, ask yourself this: "What would I say to another person struggling this way? What would I tell a friend who felt unworthy for the same reasons I do?"

Say loving, compassionate statements to yourself. Here are some ideas:

+ I am hurting.
+ It's natural to feel this way.
+ Everyone struggles sometimes, and I am only human.
+ I commit to being kind and gentle to myself during this difficult period.
+ It's okay to be disappointed.
+ It's okay to be sad.
+ I'm going to love myself through this.
+ I am imperfect, just like everyone else, but I am doing my best.

✦ I am working so hard, even though this is difficult.
✦ I'm proud of myself.

For added benefit, say your self-compassion statements while engaging in a self-care activity like during a bath or while meditating. Give yourself a neck and shoulder massage with an essential oil. Say your affirmations while taking a walk or during a yoga class. If you have a pet, cuddle with them and speak out loud to yourself in their voice. If I'm cuddling with my sweet rescue dog, Gracie, I might say, "You think I'm smart, don't you Grace? Yes, you think I have the best ideas ever. You believe in me. I'm the most brilliant human you know!" I know, it's silly. But a little silliness can make me feel much lighter when things in my life are heavy.

✦ ✦ ✦

Developing a sense of self-worth means treating yourself with kindness and compassion so you can arrive at a place of self-acceptance. You must become a dear friend to yourself. Think about your dearest friends. Do you believe they are worthy and deserving of compassion, care, and respect? I imagine you do. And are they only worthy and deserving because they are infallible? Of course not. Do you love and accept them only because they are perfect? Okay, you get where I'm going here. You love and accept your friends despite their flaws. You believe they are worthy and deserving of happiness even in their state of imperfection. You must develop this kind, accepting relationship with yourself.

I want you to be triumphant on this path. That means you will need to trust yourself and progress at a pace and in an order that makes sense on your terms. You don't have to do it my way. As you read on, ask yourself, "Am I ready to do that? What part of that am I able and willing to do now? What part feels beyond what I am ready for right now? What would I need to do first to be ready for that?" Just utilizing this approach is a practice of self-empowerment in and of itself. It's an excellent first step in saying, "I know myself, I trust myself, and I can meet my personal goals by trusting my gut and listening to my intuition."

## What's Fear Got to Do with It?

I know I just said to trust yourself, and I want you to do that. I also want you to push yourself and not hide behind complacency while calling it "trusting your gut." One of the scariest obstacles we must face on the path to self-love is our relationship with fear. In the next chapter we will talk about empowerment, but we can't talk about how to be empowered until we talk about empowerment's arch nemesis, fear. Fear is the single biggest roadblock to empowering yourself and living a bold, beautiful life.

Fear is going to be part of this process. You can't embark on a self-growth journey and avoid feeling fear. Fear is the emotional equivalent of growing pains. It is natural and necessary but unpleasant. The aversion to feeling fear is so strong that people often tell themselves to run in the other direction every time they experience it, without properly evaluating whether the concern is appropriate. When fear wells up inside you, I want you to take a deep breath and let it out very slowly. Then do it again. It's important to slow your autonomic nervous system (the part of your nervous system that controls involuntary processes like heartbeat and breathing) so you can stay connected to your wisdom in the face of fear. You won't see things clearly or make wise decisions if you go into a fight, flight, or freeze response. So first, slow yourself down.

After you have taken some slow, deep breaths, ask yourself, "What am I afraid of? What is the worst thing I think could happen?" People often stop themselves from playing their fear story out to the end. However, if you just give yourself permission to explore the fear, you will often learn the "worst-case scenario" isn't that big a deal.

Let's say you want to tell your boss that things aren't working for you on the job. Perhaps you were hired to make sales, and it was described to you as a forty-hour-per-week job. You've been at it for several months and have come to find that part of your work involves customer service and business development past the point of sale. You are working nearly sixty hours a week due to the extra job functions. You want to define the expectations of your role and either have work delegated elsewhere so you can stay focused on the job you were hired to do or be adequately compensated for the extra hours you put in every week.

When you think about going to your boss to make this request, your heart starts pounding. Your palms sweat, and your mouth goes dry. You can't imagine getting the words out eloquently. You just know you are going to stutter and fumble, and it is going to feel awful. You don't want to do it. Fear is telling you to stay quiet, to just tolerate the job no matter how bad it is, or to tolerate it long enough to find another job so you can cut and run. But your newfound sense of self-worth is telling you that you deserve better. So what now?

### What Are the Worst- and Best-Case Scenarios?

Take a few deep breaths. Then ask yourself, "What am I most afraid of?" Is it the fear your boss will say no? Okay, let's say she says no. Then what? Are you afraid she will treat you terribly for making the request or, worse, fire you? Okay, let's say she does. Then what? Objectively speaking, even if the worst happens—she gets upset with you and you get fired—can you live with that? I mean, obviously, losing your job would suck big-time. It might temporarily make your life really challenging. Assuming you don't have a sizable nest egg built up, it could create a period of real financial stress. I don't want to minimize that.

On the other hand, you realized after only a few months that this job is not right for you. You saw the true nature of your boss and learned that the culture of this company is not one that fits with your values or your goals for your life. In this worst-case scenario, your employment was terminated, but you didn't lose your voice. You weren't a doormat. You could feel good about speaking up for yourself, honoring your self-worth, and being brave. And honestly, what kind of tyrant fires someone just for bringing up a concern about job expectations? It's definitely not the most likely outcome.

Once you have evaluated the worst-case scenario, ask yourself what the best-case scenario might be. Maybe your boss says she didn't realize you were doing so much extra work and agrees to take some things off your plate. She may also agree to compensate you for any additional hours you put in each week. Jackpot!

Now ask yourself, "What is the most likely scenario?" Usually, the most likely outcome falls somewhere in between the worst- and best-case scenarios. Maybe she will tell you that there are bugs to work out due to the rapid growth of the company or because of a recent change in ownership. It's possible that everyone is feeling the pressure right now, and there isn't an instant solution to the problem. She might ask you to be patient and tell you there should be new staff hired within a few months to ease the burden.

In this scenario, you don't get your needs immediately met, but you do get some validation from your boss. You also establish yourself as someone who is willing to speak up, have hard conversations, and actively solve problems. You gain some respect from her, even if she seems a little exasperated. Remember, she is under a lot of stress, too, but she needs strong people on her team. By advocating for yourself, you are letting her know you are a person of strength and possibly someone she can rely on in the future.

When you slow down your process and lean into the fear rather than freezing or running away from it, you give yourself the opportunity to have a healthy relationship with fear. A healthy relationship with fear involves accepting fear as a typical human experience. You want to have a reasonable tolerance for the feeling of fear and not become overwhelmed by it because you exaggerate the experience. Fear says to you, "Danger! Stop! Retreat!" You need to say to fear, "Wait. Let's examine the situation. We might be able to handle this."

In most circumstances, you will find the worst possible outcome is that you are going to be uncomfortable for a temporary period. You will have to engage in an awkward conversation. You may have to disappoint someone or give them feedback that will be hard to hear (and hard for you to say). You may have a temporary rupture in the relationship that will need to be worked through.

These are all ordinary life experiences you can handle. The fear of discomfort is often worse than the actual pain of the feared experience. Think about how many times you have been terrified of something, and then once it's over you think, *Hey, that wasn't so bad!* Once you frame fear as a normal emotion everyone experiences, one you are capable of tolerating despite its unpleasantness, it no longer holds power over you. You can accept fear as an emotion you will feel from time to time. You can tolerate and move through it.

# Acceptance of Fear

There is profound wisdom in the acceptance of fear. Once you accept it as a natural state of being, you stop being afraid of it. That's right. You can stop being afraid of fear. Sometimes, no matter how long you wait or how much you prepare, the fear won't go away. That means you'll need to get used to doing things while feeling afraid.

Anaïs Nin wrote, "And the day came when the risk to remain tight in the bud was more painful than the risk it took to blossom." Use your new sense of self-worth to remind yourself that you deserve whatever reward lies on the other side of fear.

Self-worth can help you feel brave. Accept that there will be pain in this process and that you can choose to move forward even when you are afraid. You deserve to blossom. Make yourself a mantra. "I can do hard things." "I am brave in the face of fear." "Fear does not own me." "I eat fear for breakfast!" Whatever you must tell yourself to feel strong and capable and courageous, say it and own it.

## *Strong Despite Fear*

Listen to me now. You are powerful. You are strong. You are brave. Brave people feel fear all the time. They wouldn't have to be brave if they weren't scared. People who live big, bold, fantastic lives don't do so because they never feel fear. They do so despite their fear. They don't see fear as a reason not to do something good for themselves. They see fear as a reason to wrap themselves with warmth and understanding, give themselves a kick-ass pep talk, and get out there courageously in the name of self-love. It's time for you to be one of those people.

## Takeaways and Talking Points

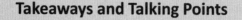

+ You are building your sense of self-worth and are well on your way toward self-love!

+ Self-worth is derived from self-acceptance, which is accomplished through the practice of self-compassion.

+ Only when we are kind and friendly toward ourselves can we accept our flaws and failures, and see ourselves as worthy of happiness despite our human shortcomings.

+ Now that you feel worthy of self-love and happiness, you must normalize and reconcile your relationship with fear. Otherwise, fear will hold you back from pursuing the life you deserve.

# CHAPTER TEN

# Empowering Your Original Self

*No star is ever lost we once have seen,*
*we always may be what we might have been.*

—Adelaide Anne Procter

O nce you have reconciled your relationship with fear and are prepared to lean into the discomfort, you are ready for Step Four. Step Four is all about empowerment. Let's start by examining what self-empowerment is and what it is not.

## Step Four: Self-Empowerment

I define self-empowerment as the condition of loving, believing in, advocating for, and honoring oneself. When we are empowered, we recognize that our needs and desires are worthy of attention, both from us and from others. We honor our needs in a way that respects us and those with whom we interact. Empowerment is powerful, but it is not rude, demanding, overbearing, or selfish. We must be careful not to bulldoze over others in the name of empowerment. I like to think of myself as a gentle warrior when I am empowered. I can stand up for myself and my needs directly and steadfastly while also being considerate and even-tempered.

## EXERCISE: WHAT'S THE OUTCOME?

Marsha Linehan is a psychologist who created *dialectical behavior therapy*, often referred to as DBT. There are four components of DBT: mindfulness, interpersonal effectiveness, distress tolerance, and emotion regulation. When practicing self-empowerment, it can be helpful to remember three questions included in the interpersonal effectiveness module. These questions are:

1. What is the outcome I seek?
2. How do I want the other person to feel about me when the interaction is over?
3. How do I want to feel about myself when the interaction is over?

Let's say I received a poor grade on a paper I put a lot of effort into. I want to empower myself to discuss it with my professor instead of cowering away from the discomfort and just accepting the poor grade. I can ask myself beforehand, "What is the outcome I seek?" Although I might have an urge to tell off the professor and let him know how harsh and unreasonable he is, that probably won't lead to the result I desire. It's essential to evaluate the ultimate desired outcome I seek, not just the feel-good urge I have. I might think, "I really want to stick it to this jerk!" But that probably isn't my true desired outcome. The outcome I genuinely hope for is an improved grade, possibly an opportunity to write revisions for a higher score, or, at the very least, increased knowledge I can take into my next writing assignment. When I keep my true desired outcome in mind, I can advocate for myself from a controlled and empowered place.

Next, I ask myself how I want my professor to feel about me after the interaction. I probably want him to see me as both intelligent and likable. Even if this is my last paper in my final semester, I don't want to burn bridges. I might need a letter of recommendation from him later, or I may apply for a job or internship with someone connected to him. I know it is essential to maintain the integrity of the relationship if I want him to work with me on the grade. I'm more likely to get my desired outcome if I conduct myself in such a way that encourages him to want to help me.

Finally, I ask myself how I want to feel about myself at the end of this interaction. If I barge, guns blazing, into his office and really tell him off, it might feel good for a moment as I discharge my upset feelings. After that initial release, I will feel embarrassed for behaving outrageously. I may have ruined my opportunity to get him to work with me, which was the outcome I really wanted. Conversely, if I go in meek and timid, and present myself as afraid and unsure, I won't leave feeling proud of my behavior either. I will probably be disappointed in myself and question what my professor must think of a student so anxious they can barely hold a conversation about a poor grade.

With all this in mind, I can decide how to approach the situation from a grounded place. I harness my wisest self to bring into the professor's office. I let him know I was disappointed in my grade because I worked hard on the assignment and my success in his class is important to me. I tell him I would appreciate his feedback to help me get a better grade on my next paper, and, if he would allow it, I would also welcome the opportunity to rewrite my assignment with the guidance of his feedback.

When I approach him in this way, I feel empowered because I present myself as competent and deserving of his assistance. I advocate for my desire to get a better grade, and I'm telling him (as well as myself) that I am worthy of the opportunity. Even if he does not allow me to rewrite the paper, I can still feel good about myself because I bravely faced my fear instead of running from it. Plus I've given myself the opportunity to learn what else he was looking for so I can improve my work going forward. I conducted myself in a professional, respectful manner and earned his respect, irrespective of the outcome. When I am empowered, I leave with a win under my belt no matter how the situation ends.

## Applying a Strength-Based Model

You might feel as though you don't have it in you yet to face difficult situations from a place of empowerment. One approach therapists employ with clients is a strength-based model. We focus on a person's inherent strength and positive attributes versus focusing on weaknesses or what isn't working.

For example, a therapist might ask at the beginning of the session, "What has gone well since the last time we met?" or "What successes have you had since our last session?" This encourages clients to notice what is working and stay motivated based on positive outcomes and forward movement, even if the progress is occurring in relatively small victories.

### *Positivity on Purpose*

The practice of *positive psychology*, a term first coined by Martin Seligman in 1998, focuses on well-being through self-acceptance, personal growth, and creating purpose. There are many practices you can engage in to begin promoting positive thought and to encourage a state of well-being. I believe happiness is an intentional practice.

Author Yehuda Berg wrote, "If you look for the bad, you will find it. If you look for the good, you will find it. We always have a choice between two realities: the positive and the negative. The reality we invest our energy in is the one in which we exist."

Essentially, both existences are accurate. The sucky parts of life are real. So are the awesome parts. As I mentioned earlier, our brains are biologically wired to focus on the negative for safety and survival purposes. To function from a place of happiness and well-being, we must be intentionally positive.

Here's the good news. Even though the negativity bias wires us to attend to the negative, we have the power to train our brains to think more positively. We have this power thanks to *neuroplasticity*, the brain's ability to change and adapt to our experiences. We can use neuroplasticity to our advantage when we use the power of our minds to create changes in our brain.

Think of it this way. No one is born knowing how to play the piano. But lots of people learn to play the piano very well by reinforcing their piano-playing skills over and over through memorization and practice. You can use this same cognitive process to be happier and kinder to yourself by attending to positive experiences with intention and by repeatedly engaging in self-loving thoughts and activities.

## EXERCISE: MAKE AN AFFIRMATION LIST

Remember the video of spunky little Jessica and her daily affirmations? I want you to make your own. You don't have to shout them out in front of the mirror every morning, though you might want to try it at least once, just for fun. At my practice, we encourage clients to write a list of positive affirmations, one for each year of their life. That means if you are twenty-nine years old, you write twenty-nine affirmations. I've instructed clients well into their seventies to do this assignment, so there are no excuses for advanced age. The way I see it, the longer you've been alive, the more strengths you have developed.

There are a few things to keep in mind when putting together your list of personal affirmations. First, you should keep them in the present tense. They should also be written in the form of "I" statements. For example,

+ I am smart.
+ I am loyal.
+ I am a good friend.
+ I have beautiful eyes.
+ I like my crooked teeth.
+ I am a good teacher.
+ I am an artist.
+ I enjoy cooking for my friends and family.
+ I have survived hard times.
+ I am doing my best in life.

Keep in mind that you don't have to believe the affirmations fully, and they don't have to be 100 percent true 100 percent of the time. For example, I wrote "I am kind" on my list, even though I know I am not always kind. I am kind most of the time, and I aspire to be a kind person, so it belongs on my list. You can also add things you are working on. If you are actively working on being a more honest person, even if you haven't been rigorously honest in the past, you can write, "I am honest" or "I am working hard to be an honest person." You might even go so far as to write, "I am trying to forgive myself for my past dishonesty and be a more honest person now and in the future."

As you add affirmations to your list, you may reach a point when you think, *I can't possibly write anymore! There aren't any other positive things about me!* If you get to this point, ask yourself, "What would my family and friends say about me? What would my pets say about me? What would God [or whatever higher power you believe in] say about me?" Step outside your self-criticism and look at yourself through the eyes of those who would be more loving and less critical of you. What would your teachers, students, children, boss, or coworkers say about you if they were instructed to list your positive attributes?

While I find writing affirmations most helpful when you focus on your innate goodness rather than your accomplishments, looking at the things you are proud of is also worthwhile. For example, I completed my undergraduate degree as a single mom of three children, who went to school full time while also maintaining a full-time job. You better believe I am proud of that. While I could put "I am educated" or "I am proud of my college degree" on my list, I might want to first think about what that accomplishment says about me. I believe it says, "I am tenacious. I am persistent. I don't give up. I do hard things. I am a positive role model for my daughters. I am a strong woman. I am powerful. I am driven. I have a great work ethic. I am determined." These are all examples of my positive attributes that are represented from a single accomplishment. Focusing on who I am at my core brings about much more pride and self-worth than merely listing my accomplishments.

## EXERCISE: SET A DAILY INTENTION

Once this assignment is complete, you need to decide what to do with your list. Some people choose to hang it in a place where they can see it every day, like a bathroom mirror or the refrigerator. You may wish to read it every morning and set an intention for the day, focusing on one or two affirmations. For instance, if one of your declarations is "I am nonjudgmental," you may say to yourself, "Today I am going to be nonjudgmental as often as possible" or "I am going to acknowledge myself with appreciation each time I am nonjudgmental toward myself today." At the end of the day, you can take a moment to journal or reflect on your successes. "Today I was nonjudgmental toward myself when I spilled coffee on my shirt. In the past, I might have been hard on myself and embarrassed, but today I was able to have compassion for myself and even laugh it off later in the afternoon. I'm really proud that I gave myself permission to be human and imperfect and didn't make a bigger deal out of it than was warranted."

In setting intentions, the goal is to intentionally focus on the successes, even if you have some challenges. If you notice yourself being judgmental toward a coworker, you don't have to beat yourself up for it. Just turn it around: "I noticed I was being judgmental toward Emily, so I shifted my thinking and offered her some help," or "When I noticed I was being judgmental toward Emily, I paused my thoughts and internally offered her compassion and wished her well." Even if you were judgmental toward something or someone during the day, try to notice the moments that you weren't. If all else fails and you really struggled with your intention, you can always say to yourself, "I acknowledge that I had a hard time not being judgmental today. I am noticing when I am judgmental and reflecting on it so I can be a less judgmental person moving forward. I'm not perfect, but I am working to become a better version of myself, and I'm proud of myself for that." Remember, you are doing your best out there. Life is hard. Personal growth is a process. Being your best self takes a lot of work. Be gentle toward yourself along the way.

## EXERCISE: KEEP A GRATITUDE JOURNAL

There are a few other positive psychology techniques I regularly use that I find particularly helpful. A personal favorite is keeping a gratitude journal. At the end of the day, write down one or even a few things that made you feel grateful. They can be things specific to the day, like "I'm grateful for the nice weather today," or "I'm grateful for the compliment my boss gave me on my latest project." It's also helpful to include the little things we often take for granted, like "I'm thankful for my strong legs that allow me to work on my feet all day," or "I'm thankful for the existence of modern transportation so I don't have to walk everywhere I need to go."

One thing I encourage clients to add to their gratitude journals is gratitude toward themselves. Every day think about what you appreciate about yourself or something specific you were proud of that day. "Today I was proud of myself when I gave a dollar to a homeless man. That was kind of me," or "I am proud that I stayed engaged with my husband in that difficult conversation and didn't shut down." Again, feel free to acknowledge the little things that are often overlooked. "I appreciate how friendly and outgoing I am," or "I really love that I am helpful and encouraging of others. That is a great quality about me." Keep in mind that some days this will be harder than others.

On really terrible days, give yourself permission to lower the bar. Remember that on any given day, you are doing the best you can. Nobody runs at their full potential every day, and you are no exception. Some days your gratitude journal entries will include versions of "I'm proud I got out of bed and brushed my teeth today," or "I'm thankful I didn't punch anyone in the face today." It's okay. We've all been there.

## The Value of Practicing Optimism

One thing I really love about positive psychology is the focus on learned optimism. You may already be familiar with the term *learned helplessness*, a condition in which one experiences a sense of powerlessness due to conditioning or traumatic experiences. A classic example is that of the young circus elephant tied down with chains to keep him from escaping, try as he might. Eventually, this sad little elephant accepts his fate and stops working to free himself. Ultimately, he can be tied up by a flimsy rope from which he could easily break free. He has been so conditioned into a state of learned helplessness that he will accept the rope as binding and will not try to free himself.

Take some time to consider the chains that held you down in the past. Have they turned into ropes? Are you accepting these ropes as chains? Many of us are operating under the presumption of helplessness in at least a few areas. It is important not to blindly accept conditions that were once true as always true. You must be willing to evaluate your current circumstances and approach your life with mindful awareness and creative problem solving. Things are not as they once were. You are smarter, stronger, and more capable today than you have ever been.

This leads back to the concept of learned optimism as a replacement for learned helplessness. The practice of learned optimism requires you to accept that happiness can be chosen and intentionally cultivated. It means we can't assume people who are happy are happy because their lives just happen to be working out swell for them. When we practice learned optimism, we acknowledge that our happiness is, in large part, our own creation, based on how we choose to perceive and respond to our circumstances. We accept that we are not powerless, and that even if our current situation royally sucks, we likely have some choice and power over it. We can use our optimism to make good decisions, respond in a healthy manner, and improve the situation in whatever way we can.

Here's an extreme example. Let's say you have been convicted of a heinous crime you did not commit. You have been sentenced to life in prison, and, despite your attorney's best efforts, all appeals have been rejected. With a heavy heart, your attorney tells you there is nothing more she can do. You will have to accept your fate: life in prison with no chance of parole.

This is a worst-case scenario come to life. You have a decision to make now. It would be easy to give up entirely, succumb to depression, be miserable and angry, and live the rest of your natural life full of hopelessness and resentment. Or you could choose to find a way to live a meaningful, happy life regardless. You could sign up for all the classes and work opportunities the prison system will give you. You could choose to mentor other inmates and be a leader in creating a better prison culture. Maybe you could even write a memoir about your experiences.

I once encountered a man in just this situation. The circumstances around his conviction were outrageous. He was in his sixties when I met him and had been in prison since he was a teen for a murder he clearly had not committed. He had been up for parole several times in his life but was denied each time. I was struck by how peaceful he was. At the end of our conversation he said to me with full sincerity, "Even though I've spent my life in prison, I've still had a good life." It was such a powerful moment for me. Prison had not hardened him. He remained a gentle soul who was well respected among both the inmates and prison staff. He was up for parole again, and I hoped so much for him that this time the system wouldn't fail him. His request was again denied. But his learned optimism allowed him to maintain a happy, peaceful heart and find a way to create meaning in his life despite circumstances that could tear a person's psyche apart.

Hopefully, the challenges you are facing today are not that dire. You probably have much more power and choice over the direction your life is going. You have a duty to yourself and the young person you once were to lead the best life you can.

## EXERCISE: SET YOUR GOALS

Think about what you want your life to look like at some point in the future. It could be six months, a year, or five years from now. Write down five goals for where you will be in your life at this determined point in the future. Maybe you will have finished your college degree, bought a house, or overcome a debilitating phobia. Perhaps you want to create a piece of art that sells in a gallery, run a 5K, or climb the Inca trail to Machu Pichu. Pick goals that are not dependent on other people, so getting married or having kids isn't a great option here. Those are lovely goals, but for this activity I want you to focus on goals that are entirely within your power alone.

Be realistic. If your goals for the next year are to get into Harvard, complete an Iron Man, and cure cancer, you might not be setting yourself up for success. I suggest including some small, more easily attained goals on your list so you can have some early success. Perhaps you want to master the advanced Lord of the Dance yoga pose or be known among your family and friends for making the most delicious lasagna ever.

Now I want you to write down one thing you can start doing right now to move one step closer to each goal. "Start stretching for ten to fifteen minutes every day," or "Sign up for a community college class," or "Start putting a hundred dollars a week into a savings account." The trick here is to balance what is attainable with what pushes you slightly out of your comfort zone. "Doable but challenging" should be your intent. Too simple and you won't benefit from the deep satisfaction derived from achieving something difficult. Too complicated and you may not achieve the goal at all.

Finally, ask yourself, "What is getting in the way of my taking this first step right now?" Use your sense of learned optimism to find creative solutions to the obstacles in your way and motivate yourself to start with small steps in a forward direction. Once you have succeeded at this first step, ask yourself, "What next step can I take now to move me closer to my goal?" If your first step toward mastering that challenging yoga pose was daily stretching, your next step could be joining a yoga studio or attending a yoga class twice a week. Keep biting off one piece at a time, even if the pace is slow and even if you sometimes take steps backward before you can move forward again.

For example, if you get a running injury, you'll need to take the proper time and steps to heal completely before getting back to your Iron Man training. But hey, the passage of time will continue no matter what. You may as well spend that time working to get yourself somewhere great. If somewhere great for you just means liking yourself more and being kinder to yourself, then that's fantastic.

Last, stay focused on what is working. Your brain will be driven to look for what is wrong. You must train it to look for what is right. I wrote earlier of shifting the question "What's wrong with me?" to "What happened to me?" Now is the time to shift "What's wrong with me?" to "What's right with me?" Identifying and harnessing your strengths is the last crucial piece of Step Four. You can't be empowered if you don't know where your power lies and how to use the power inside you. What do you like? What are you good at? Where are you having success currently? What has worked in the past? Use neuroplasticity to your advantage, and train your brain to find the positive!

## EXERCISE: TURN YOUR AFFIRMATIONS INTO ART

Turn on some music that makes you feel strong and powerful and draw out all the things that make you awesome. Draw the people who have been your personal angels: the mentors, family, and friends who have sent you messages of encouragement along your journey. Above them, write the messages they send you. For example, a picture of your favorite high school teacher might hold the message "I believe in you." That is a gift you get to carry with you for the rest of your life, even if you'll never see her again. Draw your accomplishments, big or small. Write above each one what that accomplishment says about who you are. For example, if you recently achieved your goal of bench pressing 250 pounds, the message might be "I am determined." Draw your talents. For example, if you were asked to sing at a friend's wedding, that might hold the meaning "I am valued." Keep this drawing somewhere convenient so you can reach for it whenever you need a little empowerment pick-me-up. Step Five will require you to hold on to your sense of strength as you weather the storms of self-growth.

## Takeaways and Talking Points

+ Empowerment means showing up for yourself assertively yet with respect for others.

+ You've acquired new skills for empowering yourself by getting clear about what you want, how you want others to feel about you, and how you want to feel about yourself.

+ Make an affirmation list, set a daily intention, start a gratitude journal, practice optimism, and create some impressive goals. You've got this!

## Chapter Eleven

# Become the Badass You're Meant to Be

*I got my own back.*

—Maya Angelou

H ere you are. Ready to embark on this fifth step in your very own hero's journey. If you aren't familiar with this concept, I'll give you a short review.

## The Hero's Journey

The hero's journey is a template used by writers when creating the vision for a plot. The short version is: The hero gets some sort of call to adventure, follows the call, faces obstacles (villains, perhaps), must make painful decisions, gets a little help from other travelers along the way, ultimately experiences victory, and returns home forever transformed by the experience.

You are the hero in the story of your life. You were born into this world and called to adventure. What your adventure is, I cannot say.

Perhaps you were called to create art, connect with others, be a healer or a teacher, or roam the world as a perpetual student and philosopher. Maybe your dreams involve finding a partner, creating a peaceful home, and raising a loving family. Whatever your calling, it is yours to discover and cultivate.

As I write this book at forty years of age, I realize I have received many calls to adventure. I'm not sure any of them have been my one true purpose. My life has been a kaleidoscope of experiences and callings that all seemed meaningful at the time. I think it's okay to have various missions and many adventures that change over time as you do. If you are searching for meaning in your life and you aren't sure what your "great calling" is, don't sweat it. Maybe you'll figure it out. Perhaps you'll just grow and keep evolving into better versions of yourself and find an adventure in each passing chapter of your life. That has felt productive and satisfying to me.

Back to your hero's journey. It has led you here, to a book about how to love yourself and live your best life. That in and of itself says you have been called to an adventure of self-growth. That's awesome. So far you have delved into your deep past to face down the monsters that created your insecurities and self-doubt. They might not have been real villains. Your hang-ups may have come from well-meaning but hurtful parenting techniques or from bullying from other kids going through their own hardships. You may have lived in the shadow of a superstar sibling or had a sick parent. Maybe you grew up in poverty, with underfunded schools and limited resources to create a better life.

Perhaps you had to reconcile how you were different from those around you; a dark-skinned person living in a light-skinned community, a gay person living in a straight community, or a person with disabilities living in a physically unaccommodating community. As we've already discussed, you don't have to be the victim of severe child abuse to become an adult with massive insecurities and an inability to love yourself fully. Whatever your challenges entailed, they are valid. Their impact has been real. You get to own your truth unapologetically. If you made it into adulthood, you're a survivor in one way or another.

Now, some people reading this are abuse survivors, and for those who resonate with that, I want to give you this message: Your abusers, whoever they were or are, tried to break you. But you are here, connected with these words at this moment, which means they failed. You survived, and now you have been called to build a victorious life for yourself. Though they tried to break you, they unleashed the warrior in you. You are on your hero's journey, and you are in the phase of obstacles and challenges. Like the phoenix, you will rise. I know this because I rose out of my own ashes and because I have worked with so many who rose out of theirs. You are powerful, and it is the power within you that allowed you to survive your darkest hours. It is the same power in you that brought you to this moment of reckoning. You are fighting for yourself right now, which makes you a real hero. You have not always been in a position of power in your life. Others have had control over you, for a variety of reasons that all made sense. But that time is over. It's time to take your power back. This is where the hard work of Step Five begins.

## Step Five: Self-Growth

At this point, you should have a clearer understanding of why you are the way you are. Hopefully you now feel encouraged, motivated, and empowered to change your life. Your journey has led you here: to the hard work required to reframe your thoughts and challenge the way you think about yourself, others, and the world. This step is the hardest, so this chapter is the longest. The concepts presented here get a little clinical. If you are like me and that kind of thing can be overwhelming, give yourself permission to read this chapter in small sections, or read it as often as you want to make sure you soak in all the material. Remember that the hardest parts of life are often the most rewarding, so you don't want to skim over this part of the journey.

Sometimes, when I am really struggling with the challenges life places in front of me, I like to remind myself that I have a 100 percent success rate for getting through difficult times. So far, nothing has taken me down completely. Not everything works out the way I hope or plan; sometimes I've had to abandon ship entirely, but I have survived. I have overcome. I have recovered. I rise and fall like the sun, but I never fail to rise.

## *Depending on Unhealthy Coping Mechanisms*

I must acknowledge that part of what helped me rise time and again were unhealthy coping mechanisms I developed over the years. We all fall victim to this. For instance, let's say a tired mom says no to her toddler when he asks for a treat. The toddler throws himself on the ground and begins screaming and crying. The poor, tired mom doesn't have the energy for a tantrum and hands her son the treat. What did this toddler just learn? Throwing a tantrum gets him what he wants. He just connected an unhealthy behavior to a positive outcome. What are the chances he continues to utilize this tactic? Pretty darn good.

This example highlights the way humans can come to depend on their unhelpful behaviors. That's what makes Step Five so challenging. We've reached the point of your journey where you must evaluate your own unhealthy coping mechanisms and be willing to shift out of them. Your brain will reject this notion. It will implore you to keep doing what's working. You need to critically evaluate your behavior and examine both the pros and cons of continuing certain behaviors.

Let's say you get reactive and defensive every time someone offers you feedback. That behavior probably keeps people from criticizing you, but at what cost? Others may avoid getting close to you or working on projects with you, and may talk about you behind your back. Wouldn't it be better to learn how to handle constructive criticism without defensiveness? The answer is yes, but still, it will be painful.

## Soothe Your Inner Child

Because this work can be painful, it is essential to hold on to realistic expectations as you move through your personal healing and growth process. Despite all the work I put into loving myself, treating myself with kindness, offering myself forgiveness, and practicing self-compassion, I still have moments when I feel like a loser. I doubt myself. I tell myself I'm not smart enough, interesting enough, or talented enough. The voice in my head that I know isn't mine has imprinted itself on my spirit. I have come to accept that it may never go away entirely. I choose to love myself regardless. I do not see the presence of that voice as failure or defeat. I see it as a scar that reminds me where I have been and how much I have overcome. I do my best to offer myself loving-kindness when that voice shows up.

At the risk of sounding cheesy, I like to think of it as the voice of little, hurting Heidi reminding me that she is still a part of me. She needs forty-year-old Heidi, with all her strength and wisdom, to show up and protect her. Sometimes I will internally say to her, "Hello there, sweet little Heidi. I see you. I feel your pain. I know you need me. I'm here." This helps me tap into my gentle warrior self. I can protect that young, frightened, vulnerable part of myself from a place of balance and wisdom. I can be a wise adult, soothing my insecurities and remaining focused on what is true. I am smart, I am worthy, I am capable. Also, this is hard, I am scared, and I don't know what the outcome will be. Experiencing all those feelings in unison is okay.

I know it may sound silly to talk to your inner child in that way. You might not want to do it. I understand the resistance, but I'm encouraging you to try it anyway. What's the alternative? Beating yourself up? Letting self-doubt and insecurity control you? How's that been working out?

So let's try a new approach, even if it feels awkward at first. I warned you this work would feel uncomfortable at times. However, the only way to change the way your brain thinks is to engage in new, healthier thoughts with intention.

## The Dreaded Imposter Syndrome

When I hold two truths in balance (like I am capable *and* this is hard), I am practicing my DBT skills. The term *dialectical* essentially means to hold two opposing truths in balance. Marsha Linehan uses the concept of "wise mind," which is a mindfulness practice, to teach people not to run away with their emotional fears. Instead, aim to hold your emotions and your logic in balance. We can be both smart and unsure, willing but fearful, or loving and angry. When we keep all our truths in balance, we make the best decisions.

When I was in graduate school, I must have had a million moments of uncertainty. "I'm not smart enough for this. I don't belong here. My professors are going to figure out I'm in over my head." It was the dreaded *imposter syndrome*, a psychological phenomenon in which people believe they are incapable and are going to be discovered as a fraud. Luckily, just knowing imposter syndrome was a real thing, common enough to have a name, helped me tap into my wise mind.

In the most trying moments, I said to myself, "I feel overwhelmed. I am unsure and afraid. I think the other students are having an easier time or are better at this than I am, but I don't have any concrete evidence of that. My professors would tell me if they were concerned about my work. I'm getting excellent grades and good feedback. It's normal to struggle and be scared as a grad student. I can do this. All the evidence says I'm doing fine. I just need to keep doing my best and keep moving forward." That type of wise-minded internal dialogue is essential for overcoming your self-limiting thoughts.

## EXERCISE: ACTIVATE YOUR WISE MIND

One way to build an encouraging internal voice is to ask yourself, "Is this message coming from my wise mind?" Alternatively, you can ask your wise mind a question and wait for it to answer. Again, this may sound cheesy, but the truth is, you have the answers inside you. Your wisest, most grounded self lives within you just as much as your fears and insecurities do. You can choose which parts of yourself to nurture and grow. Ask yourself, "What would my wise mind say? Can my wise mind provide any additional information to consider or challenge my inner critic in some way? What does my wise mind want me to know right now?"

## Perception Is Everything

I wrote earlier of Aaron Beck's work around cognitive distortions. His theory inspired the development of *cognitive behavioral therapy,* otherwise known as CBT. The premise of this theory is that people's perceptions of events are more powerful than the actual event; changing the way a person perceives or thinks about a situation can lead to more positivity, empowerment, and overall well-being.

Let's say, for example, you have been given a serious health diagnosis, like multiple sclerosis (MS). The prognosis for a person with this condition could be a loss of mobility and chronic pain. I knew a woman named "Lizette" who used a wheelchair due to her MS. She certainly could have given in to her negative thoughts and become severely depressed. In fact, she did experience a bout of depression after getting her diagnosis and continued to struggle some days with the limits put on her by the illness.

Most days, she carried a sunny disposition, and she chose to focus on all the things she could still do. Moreover, she celebrated herself with intention every time she was able to figure out a creative way to get things done. Lizette couldn't do all the things she used to do, but she could still do many things. She found innovative solutions for the problems she faced.

Lizette chose to look for and focus on the positive aspects of her life so she could still be a happy, fulfilled person. On the days when her emotions got the best of her, when her challenges seemed too unfair and overwhelming to manage with a smile, she practiced self-compassion. Lizette honored how hard it was to live with a debilitating disease. She gave herself permission to be angry. She cried. She reached out to friends and asked for help when she needed it. She went to a support group for people with MS who could understand and validate her feelings. She practiced loving-kindness until she felt soothed, comforted, and strong enough to shift her thinking and focus on the positive again.

Lizette's happiness was not determined by her life's situation. She accepted that her MS was beyond her control, an unwelcomed curve ball life threw at her. She made intentional choices about how to perceive her experience. She understood the emotions she felt around her illness were in large part determined by what she told herself about the experience. In other words, the meaning she attached to her thoughts dictated how she felt. If she chose to attach meaning to her illness, like "My life is over" or "I'll never be able to enjoy life now," the sadness would become unbearable. She chose instead to reject those thoughts when they surfaced and use her wisdom to replace them with more helpful, realistic ideas.

The tactic Lizette employed is called *reframing*, and it's a powerful skill for challenging cognitive distortions. Dr. Beck identified fifteen primary cognitive distortions that require awareness and intervention. An instrumental part of self-growth is understanding the cognitive distortions you engage in so you can change the way you respond to your unhelpful thoughts.

## Primary Cognitive Distortions

I think it makes sense to read this section of the book twice. First, just read through all the distortions to grasp the definitions. Then go through a second time and evaluate the ways you personally engage in each distortion. It might be helpful to rate them in order of how prevalent they are in your thought process. I've incorporated some worksheets on my website if you need help identifying or reframing your cognitive distortions. You can find them on *drheidigreen.com/worksheets*. I have also included a quiz that will help you to identify your negative core beliefs based on the type of negative thoughts you engage in. Based on your results, the end of the quiz will provide a personal healing plan for you to take advantage of. Remember, you can only grow if you have a deep awareness of your own dysfunction and are willing not just to acknowledge it but to actively intervene on the unhealthy parts of you.

## *Filtering*

When a person engages in filtering, they ignore all the positive aspects of a situation and focus only on the negative, essentially filtering out the positive. Suppose someone is coming to terms with the death of a pet. They might tell themselves, "I'll never love another animal as much as I loved Buster. I'll never be as happy as I was with him in my life, and I'm never going to enjoy hiking or camping ever again because those were things we loved to do together."

Staying focused on these thoughts keeps the grieving pet owner from acknowledging the positive truths that simultaneously exist with the negative. "Buster lived a long, happy life. We brought each other a lot of joy and were lucky to have each other. I'm so glad I was able to give him so much happiness because he sure did the same for me. I have many beautiful memories of us together that I can hold on to for the rest of my life. I will remember those times with fondness whenever I hike our favorite trails or camp at our favorite spots."

Acknowledging the positive doesn't take away from the negative truths. A person grieving their pet is entitled to all their sad feelings. In fact, it's healthy to feel their sadness fully so they can grieve appropriately and move on. However, if the grieving pet owner filters out all the good because of their pain, they both perpetuate and magnify their suffering and lose the opportunity to honor the life of their beloved pet.

## *Polarized Thinking*

Also known as black-and-white thinking, this all-or-nothing way of looking at a situation removes all the nuance that exists in the world. Let's say a woman introduces her date to one of her girlfriends. During the interaction, her friend makes a teasing comment, and the woman is embarrassed. She might say to herself, "I can't believe Kiana made fun of me like that in front of my date. She was trying to sabotage my potential relationship! She is so two-faced and untrustworthy! I can't be her friend anymore."

While it's possible that this is a toxic friendship that needs reevaluation, it's also possible that the friend used poor judgment and didn't mean to be as hurtful as she was. Alternatively, the hurt friend may have been overly sensitive, taken the comment out of context, or misinterpreted the meaning. The truth about all human relationships is that they are imperfect because they involve imperfect humans.

We all hurt people we love. We say things we regret and do boneheaded things sometimes. It doesn't mean we are bad friends or bad partners. It means we are fallible beings who need to right our wrongs from time to time. If we cast off every person who ever hurts us as toxic or unsafe, we will end up very much alone. We will face a similar outcome if we fail to acknowledge the ways we show up as toxic in our relationships. It's important to examine the gray in all situations so as not to fall into black-and-white thinking.

A healthier reframe for this situation might be, "Kiana really hurt my feelings with that comment. I need to discuss it with her and find out what she was thinking. I want to share my hurt in a nonaccusatory way so she can understand my point of view and honor my feelings. I care about this friendship, so I want to handle this appropriately and come to a resolution we both feel good about."

## Overgeneralization

This faulty line of thinking happens when we take one situation and generalize it broadly across all conditions. We are all guilty of this on occasion. I once heard someone say, "I dated a guy from New Jersey. He cheated on me. Never trust a guy from Jersey. They're all woman-izers." Whoa, slow down there, cowboy. It's natural for our brains to want to categorize things. It goes back to our survival instincts. Our brains desire efficiency, and the primary goal is to keep us alive. The most efficient way to categorize is to throw everything into "safe" and "unsafe" boxes so we can quickly move on and keep up that important business of staying alive.

There is a problem with this primitive categorization system, though. We are no longer cavemen trying to avoid death by lion attack or consumption of a poisonous berry. Our brains want to categorize and move on quickly. Lion? Run! Puppy? Cuddle! Poisonous berry? No! Cheesecake? Yes, please! Guys from Jersey? Hang on a minute. The nuances of life in the twenty-first century are lost on our rep-tilian brain's categorizing system. As such, we must work at training our minds not to rashly throw situations or people into the "unsafe" box based on one experience. This is good news for guys from Jersey, and for all of us.

## Jumping to Conclusions

This distortion is exactly what it sounds like. When we jump to con-clusions, we assume we know the outcome or the truth of something without having all the evidence. We are all guilty of this, and I am no exception. I've had trouble sleeping my entire life. My husband begged me for years to get a sleep study or see a sleep specialist. I stubbornly refused because "I knew" all they would do is prescribe me a strong sleep medication that I did not want to take. Finally, after years of suffering (my own and my husband's—I'm not cute when I'm cranky), I made an appointment with a sleep specialist and was pleasantly surprised at all the non-pharmaceutical options provided to me. Being so sure I already knew what would happen when I lacked adequate data to support my theory caused me years of unnecessary sleeplessness.

## Catastrophizing

This cognitive distortion is believing something is far worse than it actually is, like making a mountain out of a molehill. The examples here are endless. You said something embarrassing when you met your girlfriend's parents for the first time, so you are convinced they hate you and your girlfriend is going to break up with you. You forgot to do something your boss asked you to do, so now you are sure you will be fired. You got a bad grade on a test, so now your dreams of getting into an Ivy League school are shattered.

This way of thinking is unhelpful in every way. How is obsessive thinking going to help the situation at all? We already discussed how worst-case scenarios usually do not come to fruition. Spending all your mental energy hyperfocused on the worst possible outcome isn't preparing you for what will most likely happen. Instead, ask yourself, "What is the most likely outcome?" Spend your energy creating a plan for the most likely scenario. Better yet, rather than obsessing about the possible worst-case scenario, ask yourself, "What went well? What could go right?" If you struggle to do this on your own, ask a trusted friend. It's often easy to see things with perspective when we aren't emotionally invested. If necessary, let someone else serve as your barometer until you get good at holding reality in balance on your own.

## Personalization

This is a distortion in which people believe they are personally responsible for outcomes when they aren't. A more amusing example of this is the superstitious sports fan. You know them; maybe you are one. They believe they must wear a specific clothing item or watch the game in a precise location for their team to win.

In more distressing situations, a person may believe they caused a negative chain of events through their behaviors or thoughts. "If only I would have answered the phone when she called. Then we would have talked for ten minutes, she would have left the house ten minutes later, and she wouldn't have been in that car accident." This example highlights how much responsibility we can assign ourselves for situations that honestly have nothing to do with us.

I can't possibly believe I have the power to make significant events occur or not occur through my simple behaviors (such as taking a call or not). The world is a jumbled-up place with things happening or not happening at random all the time. I'm just a tiny piece of the puzzle. I don't control much. I'm not responsible for happenstance. Good things happen. Bad things happen. I'll make myself miserable if I link all my actions to the bad things that happen around me.

## Control Fallacy

If personalization assigns us responsibility, the control fallacy assigns us power. A person engaging in this distortion may believe they have more control over people or situations than they do. They may also assign power inappropriately to someone else.

Let's say a married couple is arguing. Jeanine is getting really worked up because Mary is criticizing her in an elevated tone. Jeanine gets so upset she throws the remote control she is holding, and it breaks. Then she shouts, "You make me crazy! I wouldn't have done that if you weren't yelling at me!" No, girl. Mary didn't make you crazy. You let yourself get crazy.

We all choose how to respond to adverse situations. If Mary takes on responsibility for her partner's actions, she is falling victim to the control fallacy. Mary can and should own that yelling at her wife was not healthy or productive. But she didn't make Jeanine throw and break the remote. Jeanine alone is responsible for how she responded to Mary's unhealthy yelling behavior.

### *Fallacy of Fairness*

This one is pretty straightforward. Life is not always fair. If you are completely hung up on things being fair all the time, you are setting yourself up to be both unhappy and resentful. To move through life with peace of heart, you must anticipate that things will happen to you that aren't always fair.

Sometimes it will work out in your favor, like if you run a red light but don't get in an accident or get a ticket. Lucky break. The laws of fairness let you off the hook this time. Other days, you will follow the letter of the law, and another driver will randomly swerve out of his lane, sideswipe you, and speed away, leaving you on the side of the road with your damaged vehicle.

That last example is a true story from my college days. If I had been hung up on how unfair it was, I would have made a bad situation worse. Yes, it was unfair. I wasn't doing anything wrong, and I didn't deserve it. They never caught the guy, and he got away with it. The whole thing sucked. Sometimes life sucks. I accept that life sucks sometimes, and occasionally bad things that I don't deserve will happen to me. This attitude allows me to deal with the situation and move on with my life as quickly as possible without fixating on the unfairness and dragging out my own misery.

## Blaming

Okay, time for total transparency. My hit-and-run story didn't end there. When the jerk who hit me sped off, I called 911 and started chasing him in my damaged vehicle. Obviously, this was a terrible idea. All hopped up on adrenaline and youthful determination, I was resolved to get his license plate. The 911 officer told me at least twice to stop chasing him before I finally did.

Thankfully my wits came back to me, and I pulled into a residential neighborhood and stopped my car. I worked with the 911 officer to help the police find my location, and I made an official report. I was so angry about the whole thing. Can you imagine what might have happened if I hadn't settled down and followed the 911 officer's instructions? I might have caused an accident, hitting another innocent person. If I had, it would have been so easy to blame the hit-and-run driver. "He made me get in an accident!" I might have said with indignation. But that wouldn't be the truth.

The unidentified driver may have swerved into my lane, hit my car, and left me stranded, but I was responsible for my reactions. I could only blame him for what he did, not for what I chose to do in response. I'm thankful the situation wasn't worse than it was, and I got an important reminder about blaming and accountability that night.

## Shoulds

Perhaps you've heard the phrase "Stop shoulding on yourself." This speaks to all the unspoken and sometimes arbitrary rules we assign ourselves and others. When we hold the world accountable for all the rules we make up in our heads, we set ourselves up to be disappointed and unhappy.

"He should have known I would want to be invited to poker night." "I should have checked the tires before leaving on that road trip." You can should yourself and the world to death, but the truth is, we are all just imperfect people doing our best and being imperfect all the time. We aren't going to be perfect at following our own rules, and others aren't going to be perfect at it either. To be truly happy, we must accept imperfection and be willing to roll with the punches when we falter or when others disappoint us.

Shoulds aren't just about perfectionism. Sometimes they are more about the rules we create that don't make any sense. There is value in asking where our rules come from and questioning ourselves when our standards lack logic. Think about the old, unspoken rule that men shouldn't stop to ask for directions. How does that make any sense? "I'm a man, so I should be able to figure out where I'm going without directions." Says who? What does being a man have to do with geography? When we question the basis for our internal rules, we may find that some of our shoulds are pretty silly. How many times have you said to yourself, "I should have known better?" How could you when you have no prior experience?

### *Emotional Reasoning*

Emotional Reasoning is the faulty belief that our feelings are facts. "I feel unsure about this work project, so I must have done a terrible job." "I feel fat in this outfit, so I must look hideous." "I feel hurt by my brother's words, so he must not care about me." Say it with me now: "Feelings are not facts." They are just feelings. No matter how real something feels, intensity alone does not make it true.

Checking the facts is paramount to living in balance. Your brother's words may have hurt you, but what is the evidence that he doesn't care about you? Has he made you feel cared about in the past? What about the time he gave up his weekend to help you move, or hopped on a plane to be there for the birth of your first child? We can't live in a vacuum with our feelings. It's important to acknowledge our current feelings while also tempering them with all the information we have gathered about a person or situation along the way.

### Fallacy of Change

In this cognitive distortion, we tell ourselves we could be happy if other people would only behave differently. You know, if my boyfriend was more considerate, or my boss was more understanding, or if only my ex-wife were more reasonable about co-parenting issues, then I could finally be happy. Sorry, this is a hard nope.

The fallacy of change is faulty thinking because in it, you give all your power away to some other person. You hand your happiness over to someone else in hopes they will nurture and grow it for you. The problem is, it isn't their job. They are busy trying to nurture and develop their own happiness. You must take that power (and responsibility) right back into your own hands.

Part of what I do in my practice involves contracting with the family court. I work with parents to sort through co-parenting issues. One thing this work has taught me is that you must figure out how to be happy despite people in your life who might be actively seeking to irritate you. It is helpful to acknowledge, "This part of my life is extremely upsetting and annoying, but I can focus my attention on these other parts of my life that are working out well and derive my happiness from them."

Even in those moments when it feels like everything is falling apart, there are still a few things you can hold on to that bring you happiness. Remind yourself with phrases such as "At least I can go to the park and feed birdseed to the ducks. That makes me happy," or "Thank goodness for my friendship with Jamal. I don't know what I would do without him." Remember that counting on other people to show up differently is always a recipe for disappointment. You are more likely to find happiness when you value what others bring to your life despite their flaws.

In a hostile situation where you are stuck with someone for a while (like in co-parenting), seek out relationships in which you don't feel so perpetually unhappy. Focus on those healthy relationships, and don't let the annoying ones have so much power over your well-being. It feels pretty good when someone really wants to make you miserable and you refuse to let them.

### Global Labeling

When a person engages in global labeling, also known as mis-labeling, they take generalization to the extreme. Let's say you are baking your best friend a cake for his birthday. You follow the recipe step-by-step, but for some unexplainable reason the cake doesn't rise, it tastes weird, and it's not attractive to look at either.

A person who doesn't engage in any faulty thinking might laugh and say, "Welp, that was a disaster! It's the thought that counts, right?" A person engaging in generalization might say, "Well, I just can't bake. I'm never attempting a cake again!" But the person who engages in global labeling may go right to an extreme response, like, "I am a total failure. I can't do anything right. I literally suck at everything I do!"

In a moment of extreme reactivity such as this, it is helpful to employ self-compassion skills before jumping into checking the facts. When you have an emotionally charged response, practicing compassion can soften your experience of yourself and make you more open to utilizing your healthy coping skills. "Wow, I'm really upset about this. I wanted so badly to do something special and have it turn out well. I'm really heartbroken because this didn't turn out as I'd planned. I put a lot of effort into this, and my disappointment is overwhelming. It's acceptable to feel this way. It's okay to be upset when I want something badly, I work hard to make it just right, and it doesn't end up at all as I'd hoped. It's reasonable to be upset by this." Once you have calmed yourself with self-compassion, then you can check the facts, reach out to a friend, or employ another helpful coping skill.

### Always Being Right

You probably don't need to read a self-help book to tell you why always needing to be right is an unhealthy way to do life. If you put your need to be right above the health and quality of your relationships, you are setting yourself up for a life of loneliness. People who are only able to see the world through their own point of view and who aren't willing or able to admit when they've screwed something up aren't a joy to be around.

For some, the need to always be right may be the result of permissive parenting and being a child who always got whatever they wanted. They never learned to compromise, accept the boundaries of others, or consider another person's needs and feelings. For others, the need to be right may come from a deep-seated place. Maybe when you were a child, no one valued your opinions or believed you when you said bad things were happening. As a result, you grew into an adult who is adamant about always being listened to and taken seriously. That makes sense. Even so, it's no way to live your life now if you want to have healthy relationships with others.

Try to soothe that young part of yourself in those moments. "Hey there, little [insert your name here], I know you want to be heard. I know it feels terrible when people don't listen to you and agree with you. It feels a lot like long ago when you were terrified and helpless and none of the adults around would step in to protect you. It's okay. I'm here now. Today is not like then, and this situation is different from that situation. Today we don't have to insist on always being right. We can compromise and see other points of view and still get our needs met."

Engaging in an inner dialogue to soothe that young, activated part of you can help get your wise adult self back online so you can engage with others more constructively. Honestly, the need to always be right is childish. If this is a problem for you, you need to look at the wounded child within you and heal that pain so you can show up in your life today as a healthy adult.

### Heaven's Reward Fallacy

This is the final cognitive distortion. You can conceptualize heaven's reward fallacy as an expectation that you should always get a payoff for any sacrifice you make. "I worked every Saturday for six months to buy my teenager his first car! How dare he be disrespectful and stay out past curfew!" Well, because he is a teenager, and they are pretty much known for being careless, disrespectful, and selfish on occasion. That is less a reflection of his love and appreciation for you and more a reflection of his underdeveloped prefrontal cortex, which results in impulsivity and poor judgment.

The moral of the story is, you aren't always going to get your just deserts in life. Sometimes you will sacrifice much and the rewards will be handsome. Sometimes they won't. Just like the fallacy of fairness, if you always expect your sacrifices to be met with substantial rewards, you will end up being disappointed. Being prepared for things to not always work out perfectly in your favor is an excellent way to stay peaceful about a variety of outcomes. That's not to say you shouldn't be hopeful. I want you to hope for wonderful results. I also want you to be flexible and not so fixated on specific outcomes that you can't be happy when life gives you different results.

✦ ✦ ✦

Changing your cognitive distortions and the unhealthy behaviors driven by those distorted thoughts is probably the hardest part of the self-growth process. As I've already discussed, those coping mechanisms developed because they worked, and they are probably still working in some capacity. The problem is that they also have led to undesirable consequences. Self-growth requires self-awareness, and self-awareness can be painful.

## EXERCISE: CREATE A COST-BENEFIT ANALYSIS

An excellent way to begin shifting your cognitive distortions is to write out a cost-benefit analysis. Identify the cognitive distortions you engage in the most. Again, you might want to order them from most problematic for you to least problematic. Then, for each distortion, write out the thoughts and behaviors you engage in that are driven by the distortion. Finally, create two columns, one for costs and one for benefits.

Consider first what the benefits are for engaging in this behavior or holding on to this way of thinking. There is a reason you have developed a habit of thinking and behaving this way. What is it? How has it worked in meeting your needs? Get clear about how it has helped you or tricked you into thinking it was helpful. Examples might be, "When I act helpless, others make decisions for me," or "My aggressive behavior keeps people from challenging me," or "I don't risk getting hurt by others when I keep them at arm's length."

Next, examine all the ways this thought or behavior is hurting you. What is the cost of thinking/behaving this way? How has it already been harmful? How might it create more harm in the future if you don't shift gears? Seeing your challenges physically listed this way can be powerful and may just provide the clarity you need to motivate real change. For example, you may not get hurt by others when you keep them at arm's length, but at what cost? You miss out on positive interactions and meaningful relationships. You rob yourself and others of joy, laughter, fun, intimacy, companionship, and belonging. You spend more time than necessary being alone and lonely, and you're missing out on the human experience. That's a profound cost.

Once you can identify, challenge, and intervene on your unhelpful processes, you are ready to move on to Step Six. While the hallmark of Step Five is shifting out of unhealthy ways of thinking and behaving, Step Six is about mastering healthy ways of being. We can't just move out of our old ways without having a strong sense of healthier ways to live. Step Six will guide you through replacing your disrupted ways of being with health, wisdom, and acceptance.

## Takeaways and Talking Points

✦ Whew! You are braving the most challenging course on the path to self-love. Self-growth means examining our own dysfunction with candidness and a willingness to change.

✦ We have explored the fifteen most common types of cognitive distortions along with skills for reframing them.

✦ Soothe your inner child, activate your wise mind, check the facts, and create a cost-benefit analysis.

✦ If you need more help, check out my website for worksheets on identifying and challenging your faulty ways of thinking.

## Chapter Twelve

# Treat Yourself Like the Rockstar You Are

*Searching in all directions with one's awareness, one finds no one dearer than oneself.*

—Buddha

I just promised you wisdom and acceptance and started this chapter with a Buddha quote, so I suppose now is as good a time as any to talk about inner peace. What an elusive concept. What is it? Who has it? How do you get it and keep it in a world full of stress and responsibility and heartache and tragedy? We can't all go to the mountains of Tibet and breathe cold mountain air and spend several hours a day in silent meditation. I have real-life issues that need my attention. I have bills to pay and kids to cart around. My house is a mess. My car is a mess. My job is demanding. Absolutely nothing in my life is conducive to living in a state of inner peace. So how do I do it?

Well, sometimes I don't. First rule of inner peace: You aren't always going to feel peaceful. Sometimes you are going to be totally frazzled.

You will still have moments of anger and frustration and the occasional complete meltdown. For me, part of being internally peaceful is accepting that those moments are going to come. When they do, they will feel awful, but I know I will get through them and that eventually those terrible moments will pass and be replaced by better moments. That is one thing I can count on. Nothing I feel is ever permanent. No beautiful moment, no terrible moment, no feeling of bliss, no sense of agony. Every experience and sensation and emotion we ever encounter is fleeting.

## Step Six: Master a Healthy Way of Being

When I understood that everything in my life is temporary, it gave me the freedom to accept both the good and the bad without attaching myself to it. Knowing that the hard times are impermanent gives me the strength to endure them. Remembering the good times are temporary allows me to be fully present in those moments so I can appreciate them wholeheartedly. This is how I practice a concept known as *radical acceptance*.

## Radical Acceptance

Radical acceptance is the practice of accepting everything in your life as it is. People increase and perpetuate their suffering when they refuse to accept reality. You refuse to accept reality when you stay focused on what should be or what should have been. People who accept things as they are experience less suffering. They acknowledge that pain is a part of life, and they don't catastrophize when it happens. They ride it out like a ship on a stormy sea, knowing the pain exists, but also that it is not forever. It's uncomfortable, maybe miserable, but it's also temporary. People who reject what is suffer considerably more because, frankly, the energy required to deny your reality is all-consuming and exhausting.

If I get a speeding ticket on the way to work, I can dwell all day on how I should have driven more slowly or how the officer should have been more understanding. However, obsessing about what should have been won't change the situation. I can accept that I got a ticket on the way to work, acknowledge that it's a total bummer, but not allow it to ruin my whole day. I can choose radical acceptance, move on, and have a good day anyway. The result is the same in both cases because I have no control over the outcome. Although in one case, I suffer all day, and in the other, I don't. I'm not really into perpetuating my own suffering, so that's why I love radical acceptance.

### Radical Acceptance Doesn't Mean Being a Doormat

As important as it is for your emotional well-being not to fight against reality, it is also important to identify when your circumstances are unacceptable. People who practice radical acceptance are not pushovers. They do not ignore their needs or fail to advocate for themselves. They merely know which battles to fight and how to respond in a healthy way when things are outside their control.

For example, if you are in a relationship with a person who treats you terribly, radical acceptance does not say, "Well, this is just reality. There's nothing I can do about this abusive behavior, so I just have to accept it." Radical acceptance does say, "I cannot control this other person's behavior. I cannot change them." It also says, "I don't have to take it." This means you must let go of trying to convince the person to treat you differently. Instead, you accept that their behavior is abusive and that you cannot change it. You recognize you must act to protect yourself from abusive behavior, even if it means doing something you don't necessarily want to do, like end the relationship.

Now you don't want to be dramatic and cut off every relationship you have any time someone treats you in a hurtful way. You have options, but all your options involve controlling yourself and not controlling the other person. You can tell the person why what they did upset you and ask them to change their behavior. If this is a healthy person who cares about you, it shouldn't take too much more than that. You can set up boundaries and expectations for how the relationship should function in a way that respects you both. If a person is making apparent, concerted efforts to honor your boundaries, even if they are imperfect along the way, that's probably worth working through.

If you have made your needs known, set clear boundaries and expectations, and the person continues to ignore them, you must accept this is who they are. This is how they are going to treat you. If you find their behavior unacceptable and don't want to be engaged with a person who treats you like that, then you must do the only thing you have the power to do: leave.

I can control only myself. My behaviors, reactions, attitudes, and choices are all entirely within my control. Everything else is outside my control, and I must accept what is outside of me. Adopting this attitude has led me to the most peace I have ever had in my life.

Here is an example of how I used radical acceptance recently. My husband and I bought our first home together this year. During the moving process, I waited to move a few of the most valuable things I own until the very end. I was exhausted by the time we were putting together the last car full of items. I finally had the very last box to move in my arms. It was a small box, and I didn't tape it up properly.

I was going to be extra careful with it, after all. I triumphantly walked down the stairs of our rental home, took one last look at the place, and closed the door for the last time. As I went to put the box into my car, I tripped, and the contents of the box went flying.

I kept some of my most sentimental jewelry in a ceramic dish my youngest daughter made me when she was little. It was near the top of the box, and it shattered into pieces when it hit the concrete driveway. I was immediately overcome with grief. Every milestone Delaney passes is bittersweet for me because it's always "the last time" one of my girls will do something. The last band concert, the last day of elementary school, the last precious ceramic dish with the word "Mom" painted onto it. I went back into the house and sat on the stairs and had a good cry. Then I went back out to the driveway, picked up all the broken pieces, put everything back into the box, and drove to my new home. It wasn't until the next day that I remembered my wedding ring was also in that dish.

My husband and I returned to the house in the morning and scoured the driveway, front yard, and street for my ring. We came back on several occasions throughout many days to try again. I posted a picture of the ring on my neighborhood Facebook page. All our efforts were in vain. Jason and I didn't have much money when we got married. My ring, while made of real gold, was full of cubic zirconium diamonds and wasn't worth much. I think we paid a few hundred dollars for it from an online jeweler almost a decade prior. We certainly didn't have insurance for it and probably couldn't replace it. I don't even remember what website we used to buy it.

The fact of the matter became clear. It was gone. My daughter's last childhood gift to me and my beloved wedding ring were both gone in an instant. I grieved. I controlled what I could. I looked for my ring. I tried to find a replica on the internet. I glued my daughter's ceramic dish back together. Later, we bought another ring that I thought was lovely, but it wasn't the same.

I accepted that no ring will ever hold the sentiment of the ring Jason slipped on my finger the day we vowed to love each other for the rest of our lives. Nothing will fully repair the sweet little dish Delaney made me to its original form. I grieved, but I accepted that the ring was gone and the dish was broken. Accepting allowed me to grieve without undue suffering.

I didn't replay the moment I tripped over and over in my mind. I didn't beat myself up for not being more cautious, for not securing the box by taping the lid. I learned a lesson. I'll be more careful in the future. But no matter how much I torture myself over what I "should" have done differently, it will never change what is. So I accepted reality, and I grieved. I still grieve when I look down at the new ring on my finger. I grieve when I see the broken dish. But because I accept reality, I do not suffer. Moreover, I have made myself open to the idea that some-day my new ring may have its own special meaning in my life's story.

The concept of radical acceptance is fairly simple, but the learn-ing process isn't always easy. I've been practicing radical acceptance for a long time, so I've gotten good at it. I have trained my brain to be accepting and kind toward myself. I'm not always accepting and kind, to be sure. But I'm better at it now than I have ever been. When I first started practicing radical acceptance, it was hard. Sometimes I thought it was stupid. I tried to be accepting, but it felt contrived, and I got angry. If you find yourself feeling frustrated or annoyed as you begin this practice, try to remember that it's to be expected. Any time you want to train your brain to function in a new way it is going to feel weird, wrong, awkward, and/or unhelpful. I promise that you can teach yourself healthier ways to operate if you stick with it through the initial challenge.

I like to use a skill called the *third person tool*. I think about someone I love and what I would want for them if they were in my shoes. If it were Delaney who dropped the box, I wouldn't scold her repeatedly for days. I wouldn't want her to shame and condemn herself forever. With that in mind, I can offer myself the same love and understanding I would give to her. That's how you train your brain to be more loving and accepting toward yourself.

The power of radical acceptance is that it allows you to exist without judgment of a situation. That is, you have the ability to view your emotions as neither good nor bad and accept that they just are. In my last example, my grief was painful, but it wasn't wrong or bad. It was a healthy part of saying good-bye. For me, practicing radical acceptance is a primary component of living in peace.

Another instrumental part of inner peace for me is living without judgment of myself or others. I think this can be remarkably hard for people, especially those of us living in American culture where we are constantly encouraged to compare ourselves to others. So let's talk about this culture of judgment we live in.

## The Judgment Trap

I'll kick off the conversation with this: People who love themselves root for everyone. I can't be more precise than that. People who are self-loving are not jealous or toxically competitive. They don't hope others will fail so they can feel better about themselves. They don't look for reasons to condemn the looks or behaviors of others so they can feel "better than." People who love themselves know there is enough room for all of us to be happy and prosperous. There is enough love and joy in the world for all of us to have our fill. I don't need to cut anyone down, minimize anyone's accomplishments, or downplay another person's greatness to feel or be great myself.

In fact, I've spent considerable time throughout this book referring to the greatness of others. I direct you to the work of people I admire because I'm appreciative of those smarter and more experienced than I am. I have learned from those intelligent, experienced people and have built upon what they taught me to improve myself and help my clients love themselves and lead happier lives. When I keep my heart open and welcoming to the light of others, I get to reap the full benefit of their greatness, and I can be inspired into my own greatness. That feels so much better than living in the darkness of jealousy, resentment, and self-importance.

Another great mind I admire is Brené Brown. In her book *Daring Greatly*, she explains how people are most judgmental when they feel inadequate. She discusses the way mothers criticize other moms for their parenting, not because they are convinced they are perfect mothers themselves, but because they know they aren't. When a mother feels insecure about her parenting, she may feel compelled to judge the actions of other moms to feel "good enough" by being "better than." If I love and trust myself, if I know I am a great mom (even though I am a totally imperfect mom), then I don't care if you breast- or bottle-feed, use cloth or disposable diapers, homeschool or public-school your kids, and so on. I don't need to put myself above other women to feel adequate. I do me. You do you. I'm rooting for us both.

I listened to a psychiatrist give a keynote speech once in which he shared how he processes his own judgment. He said that when he realizes he is being critical toward himself or another person, he pauses and notices his internal process with curiosity. When a person is engaging in a judgmental thought, they will often do one of two things with it. They may choose to accept the idea as truth and open the floodgates for more judgment. They might say something like "Look at that woman in those nasty sweatpants. Did she even brush her hair before she left the house? I would never let myself go out like that." Or they may immediately be critical of themselves for having the judgmental thought. *Ugh, I am such a jerk! This lady is just living her life! Why do I have an ugly thing to say about everyone? I can't stand myself sometimes*. Taking the third approach, curiosity, allows you to do something different. You might say to yourself, "That's interesting. I'm having a judgmental thought about that person right now. I wonder what that's about for me."

We can engage in curiosity when we are critical toward ourselves, too. Let's say I notice the thought, *I can't believe I said that! I'm such an idiot!* I have a few options. I can accept the thought as truth: *That was idiotic. Everyone must think I am a complete moron. I'm never going to show my face here again!* I can beat myself up for it: *Dammit, Heidi! Stop talking to yourself like that! You will never master self-love if you keep being such a miserable cow!* Or I can embrace the thought without judgment and with curiosity: *Well, that's interesting. I'm being unreasonably hard on myself right now. I wonder what is going on with me. I must be feeling really vulnerable and insecure.*

This third option allows me the opportunity to come to myself with compassion for my insecurity, the way I would for a friend experiencing that same level of self-doubt and anxiety. It allows me to approach myself with words like "Hey, Heidi, you're doing fine! Was that the most eloquent thing you've ever said? Probably not. Does it mean you are a big dummy? Definitely not! I'm sure no one else thought it was a big deal. And if they did, I can always clarify later and make the situation right. I'm being brave and putting myself out there, and I am doing it imperfectly, just like everyone else. It's okay. I'm okay." In this last scenario, I practice both compassion and kindness for myself, and I accept the situation without minimizing or catastrophizing reality. This allows me to stay grounded and balanced and move on with peace in my heart.

## Embracing Imperfection

When psychologist Kristin Neff writes about self-compassion, she explains how self-compassion is an act of loving and accepting yourself despite your failures and weaknesses. This is why I dedicated an entire chapter to self-forgiveness. If I know that I can't just love myself "because of" but that I must love myself "in spite of," then I must forgive myself. In other words, I can't just love myself because I earned a doctorate degree, maintain a successful practice, and have three awesome, high-functioning, well-adjusted kids. I must love myself despite my childhood abuse, my parenting shortcomings, my failed marriage, my anxiety and self-doubt, and my hundreds of imperfections.

Brené Brown says people often falsely believe they will feel lovable or worthy "if" or "when." I will be lovable when I finally get straight A's. I will be worthy if I get the promotion. To help others combat this common but utterly false narrative, I have them build failure into their game plan. My theory here is that if you plan on struggling and plan on failing (again and again), then when you do, you're meeting your goals!

### *Prepare for Setbacks*

When clients are preparing to discharge from the PCS Intensive Outpatient Program, they are usually full of hope and optimism. While

I love to see that, I also feel I must help them recognize they won't always feel like this. I ask them, "What are going to be your biggest barriers to success? Where are you going to struggle the most? What is your plan for when things get really hard or when you have taken steps backward?" Sometimes, in their state of renewed optimism, they respond, "I don't think it's going to be that hard now to [fill in the blank: stay sober, follow my wellness plan, tell my partner the truth, etc.]." I bring them back to reality immediately. "It will be hard. So, what are you going to do when you are craving a drink, have neglected self-care, or told a lie?"

We don't have to see failure as a bad thing. Failure means we are trying. Failure means we are taking risks and putting ourselves out there. Failure means we have decided we want something meaningful and we are brave enough to go for it. So you failed. Big deal. You are light-years ahead of those who are too scared to try. (Uh oh. See what I just did there? I compared you to others, which I just told you not to do. I put others down to help you feel better about your own shortcomings. Darn. Let me try again.)

So you failed. Congratulations! You are trying! You created a dream, and you are brave enough to go for it! You must really believe in yourself to be so courageous and vulnerable out in the world. You are admirable. You are inspiring. You are strong. Big dreams are hard to chase, and repeated failing is part of the process. You are learning. You are getting smarter, better, and closer to achieving your dream with each failure. I'm proud of you. I hope you're proud of yourself. You're doing it! (Ahh. That felt right. It genuinely feels so much better to be encouraging without putting others down. I promise.)

# Self-Acceptance

All this talk of self-acceptance is great in theory, but the truth is, we live in a world that profits from our self-loathing and insecurity. So even if we are intentional in nonjudgment toward ourselves and others, even if we accept our own imperfections and failures as a natural part of the human experience, we still must survive in a media-driven society that continually bombards us with messages of our unworthiness. How are we to ever rid ourselves of the notion that we are only lovable and worthy "if" or "when" while everything in our environment is trying to convince us we are only lovable and worthy "if" or "when"?

Let's say, in a not-at-all-hypothetical example, I am a middle-aged woman in America, and I would like to love and accept myself and my body despite my deepening wrinkles and ever-growing love handles. I engage my best efforts to stay grounded in reality with statements like, "Youth and beauty are not a testament of my worth. I have value and am worthy of taking up space no matter how my physical appearance changes over time. I am physically and emotionally healthy, and beautiful in my own right. I don't look like I'm twenty-five anymore, but that isn't what is important. My body is strong, my mind is capable, my heart is good. I like who I am."

After I give myself this inspiring little pep talk, I turn on the television and see nothing but commercials for skin cream, weight loss programs, and makeup. On my way to work, I pass billboards for my local plastic surgeons and dermatologists. I hear ads on the radio for gyms promising to get me "bikini ready" for the summer. I drive past the med spa where I once (okay twice) got Botox and wonder if I need to try it again. Despite my very best intentions to send myself out into the world full of love and self-acceptance, the inundation of messages proclaiming my unworthiness is immediate and profound.

Moreover, many of these crafty advertisers are using my desire to love myself against me. I see more advertisements than I can count that relay messages that I will buy expensive skin products because "I'm worth it" or that I'll subscribe to a monthly fitness app or purchase eight-dollar bath bombs (OMG eight dollars to take one bath?!) as "self-care." I really need to keep my blinders on and stay in my most grounded headspace out in the world most of the time. I remind myself that I can still love myself if I buy cheap drugstore eye cream. Buying inexpensive skin care products doesn't mean I see myself as unworthy. I get to decide how I spend my money in a way that honors my worthiness.

Maybe I tell myself I'm worthy of world travel, so I don't spend money at the nail salon, the med spa, or on designer shoes and purses, but instead I save up to take myself on epic adventures. I take incredible pictures, meet awesome people, and create priceless memories. If that's what my heart longs for, I am worth it. I remind myself that I can go on sunset walks with my dogs, quiet morning hikes, check out a book from the library, or take long, relaxing baths, all for free. I am worth those things, too.

I can do these things and not love myself any less than the person spending considerable money on fitness and beauty. In fact, I might decide I love myself so much I'm going to skip the Botox all together and spend that money on baking beautiful, mouth watering cakes, tending a garden, or taking a pottery class if that is what brings me joy. I'm not going to deny myself any self-love activities just because commercials tell me I should be more worried about what gravity is doing to my face than anything else.

# Real Self-Care

Self-care is more than how we spend our money to look good, feel good, prove we value ourselves, or escape reality. Self-care is building a life we love, a life we don't need to escape from so often. When I remind myself that all that media-driven noise is just a ploy to take my money and make other people rich off my insecurities, it helps. It doesn't drown out the noise entirely though. So I keep moving through the world and do my best. I keep asking what brings me genuine happiness. What do I really value versus what am I told to value?

Ask yourself, "Am I surrounding myself with things I love, the things that make my life fulfilled and worth living?" If so, great. If you love the way that expensive face cream makes your skin feel, then super. If your bimonthly trip to the nail salon, your weekly bath bomb, your posh gym membership, or your designer shoes bring you real (not faux) joy, then, yes, it's worth it. If it helps you genuinely love yourself more (not just loathe yourself less), then absolutely, it's worth it. If it sends you a message that you are valuable and increases your overall satisfaction with your life, then go on with your bad self. In fact, maybe I'll get a little more Botox after all. There's no rule that says I can't love myself fully while not loving my forehead wrinkles.

Each of us must create our own value system and live within it. I can't tell you what should or shouldn't make you happy. I won't tell you what you should or shouldn't value. That makes me no different from everyone else who is trying to sell you something. You get to decide for yourself what makes your life worth living. I only want to encourage you to find those answers from deep within yourself and not from a commercial, self-comparison, or someone's insults.

Remember, self-care isn't just how we escape the stresses of our life. Real self-care is how we honor our needs, engage in what brings us joy and meaning, and create a life we love. I think this quote from artist Caroline Caldwell sums up the sentiment perfectly: "In a society that profits from your self-doubt, liking yourself is a rebellious act." It's time we all join the rebellion.

## Takeaways and Talking Points

+ You'll need to find healthy thought patterns to replace your unhealthy thoughts.

+ Radical acceptance is a practice that can help you feel more internally peaceful by accepting reality. When you practice radical acceptance, you don't try to change situations in which you have no control, and you don't agonize over how things should be different. You control what you can and accept what you can't change.

+ Another component of healthy thought is giving up the judgment of self and others. Healthy people intervene on critical, negative thoughts when they come into consciousness.

+ We need to support others and ourselves, acknowledging that at any given moment, we are all doing the best we can.

+ Finally, real self-care is essential for emotional wellness. When we practice true self-care, we enhance our lives with loving activities that align with our values.

## Chapter Thirteen

# Take Over the World

*The most important relationship*
*of my life is the one I am having*
*right now with myself.*

— Heidi Green

You've made it. This is the last step on the path to self-love and metaphorical world domination. Step Seven is all about fostering joy and purpose in your life. It is how you take everything you have learned so far, apply it to be your best self, and live your most fulfilling life.

## Step Seven:
## Foster a Life of Joy and Purpose

If you have been engaged in meaningful self-reflection throughout reading this book, hopefully you have identified how your original, true self got mangled up by life. Also, you should have a good sense of the negative and (at least mostly) false beliefs about yourself and the world you have been carrying around with you due to your painful life experiences. With that knowledge in hand, I hope you have been engaging in intentional self-compassion, self-forgiveness, and self-kindness to build yourself up the way you would for any other struggling person you encounter. As your inner strength and sense of empowerment have grown from these self-loving behaviors, I hope you have been setting boundaries, exiting toxic relationships, lifting others, eliminating self-destructive behaviors, and engaging in real self-care.

## Self-Care vs. Comfort-Seeking

I say real self-care because I want to differentiate self-care from unhealthy comfort-seeking. Dr. Daniel Sumrok, director of the Center for Addiction Sciences at the University of Tennessee Health Science Center's College of Medicine, presented one of the most compelling theories on addiction I have ever read. He postulates that addiction is the result of ritualized, compulsive comfort-seeking.

Here's the thing about compulsive comfort-seeking. People who aren't living in a chronic state of pain don't need to seek comfort compulsively. If I live in a perpetual state of internal distress, I am going to look for any source of comfort to bring me relief, even if I know it is temporary or destructive. No one can tolerate hurting all the time. Sometimes, the desire for a moment of respite from pain can drive people to do things they know aren't good for them in the long run.

Dr. Sumrok attaches his theory to the ACE study, highlighting correlations between the number of ACEs a person has and the level of chronic pain they live in, ultimately increasing their chances of becoming an addict. He advocates for addiction treatment with a focus on trauma therapy to reduce the chronic emotional pain from those old wounds. Although he focuses primarily on substance use, I think all addictions apply. Whether you compulsively seek out food, relation-ships, sex, shopping, gambling, or drugs and alcohol, the motivating factor is the same: comforting the chronic pain.

We can easily apply this theory outside the context of addiction. I like to apply his concepts to all unhealthy, comfort-seeking behaviors. Examples include overworking, emotional eating, "retail therapy," excessive exercising, obsessive video gaming, binge-watching tele-vision, or engaging in risky, adrenaline-seeking behaviors. The more socially acceptable the behavior, the more likely we are to get away with calling it "self-care."

Remember what I said earlier about self-care. The single most important act of self-care you can engage in is creating a life from which you don't feel the need to escape regularly. That means if your drive to eat, go to happy hour, shop, work, exercise, play video games, or watch TV is internally demanding, it may not be coming from a healthy place. That motivation to numb, distract, achieve, or just plain feel something might be more about comforting your chronic emotional pain than engaging in real self-care. True self-care is icing on the cake in a life that already feels satisfying and joyful. If your "self-care" seems like the thing you need to do to get through the day or tolerate your life, your job, or your marriage, it's probably not real self-care. The hard truth is, if your life sucks, no amount of massages, great workouts, chocolate, or martinis is going to fix it.

## Find Your Happy

So let's talk about creating a life worth living, the same satisfying, joyful life of which I just wrote. You've probably heard the old saying, "People who are happy don't have the best of everything, they just make the best of everything." There is a lot of truth to that. Some of the happiest people I have encountered have relatively little in the way of material possessions. They aren't rich or powerful, and they aren't always beautiful or influential. They certainly aren't perfect. They have encountered significant challenges: illness, physical disability, children with special needs, addiction, career setbacks, financial hardships, and horrible injustices. But their lives are rich with love, purpose, passion, joy, and meaningful relationships. They have defined what they value most. They are clear about what is important to them and what is just filler. They have mastered focusing on, nurturing, and engaging where it matters, and filtering out the noise of what matters less.

As I sat down to write this chapter, news broke of a celebrity suicide. I am reminded in the most sobering way of the falsehood that is "I will be lovable and worthy if/when." I am reflecting not just on those I know who are happy with so little but also those who are miserable with so much. You might achieve fame, success, money, power, respect, accolades, worldwide admiration, and all the things we tell ourselves will finally make us feel worthy and happy. And yet so many who spend their lives striving for the top find it empty and unfulfilling once they reach it.

What is the answer then? Let's be real. None of us have the answer. There are some universal truths, but most of us are just fumbling around, doing our best, trying to learn from our experiences and lead the best lives we can. I don't have the answer. But I have some good ideas. I have committed my professional life to studying and working with people, to understanding human psychology and interpersonal relationships. I have developed expertise in treating mental illness and fostering emotional wellness. I've witnessed scores of people move out of sickness and into happiness. And I've done it myself. So let's look at what I've seen work.

## EXERCISE: DEFINE YOUR VALUES

First, I think it is imperative to define your values. What matters to you most? What elements of life are a requirement for you to feel fulfilled? I suggest you make a values list. Think about what is underneath each value. For example, if you put "becoming a father" as a value, what is it about parenthood that is so important to you? Be clear about it. That way, if you don't become a father, it doesn't become a source of despair. Perhaps the value underneath your desire to be a parent is you want to love and be loved, or you want your presence, guidance, and wisdom to be meaningful to others. Maybe you value mentorship and want to help others achieve their dreams. Parenthood is a natural source for integrating these values into your life, but it isn't the only way.

Once you have whittled down to the purest elements of each value on your list, ask yourself, "What are all the ways I can incorporate this value into my life? How can I start incorporating these elements right now?" Don't wait until after you have a college degree, get that dream job, get married, have a specific dollar amount in your bank account, or whatever other limitation you put on yourself to keep that "if/when" fallacy thriving in your head.

Do you value travel and adventure? Great. Take a weekend road trip. Go camping. Try geocaching. Find out where all the best hikes or views or lakes are in your state and go see them. Drive to the nearest beach and make yourself a sand castle. Check out some quirky mom-and-pop restaurants in your area owned by people from countries you would like to visit. You don't have to wait until you have the time and money to backpack through Europe to start enjoying and exploring the world around you.

Do you value learning? Take a class at a community college.

Find some great podcasts or books on subjects interesting to you. Check out the museums in your area. Make a commitment to yourself to learn something you've always wanted to learn. Pick up an instrument or a foreign language. Learn to cook or paint or build furniture or repurpose old household items. You don't have to get a college degree to learn. You don't have to commit twenty hours a week to a learning endeavor. You can invest two hours a week. You can commit fifteen minutes a day. Do whatever makes sense in your life, and don't completely avoid doing something that would enrich your life just because you tell yourself you don't have time to do it perfectly.

Do you value meaningful relationships? Wonderful. Take stock of the relationships you already have. Are they fulfilling? Fun? Do they make you feel good about yourself? Do you feel honored, valued, and cared about? If not, decide what you can control. Try to improve relationships you want to salvage by setting boundaries and asking for your needs to be met. Give yourself permission to let go of relationships that are harmful. Even if you have already invested a lot of time and energy into them, even if they are blood relations, you are never obliged to people who make you feel like crap.

Find your people. Join a meet-up group or a book club, find a place of worship that jibes with your soul, or join a community group on Facebook. Can't find the kind of group you are looking for? Start it! A friend of mine started a group for women with young kids who wanted to exercise together. She posts pictures on social media all the time now with her mom friends going on stroller runs with their littles or stretching at the playground. It's adorable. Take a class at your local community center. Offer to teach a class at your local community center. Audition at your local community theater or offer to be a part of the production team. Volunteer at a local nonprofit that does something you feel passionate about. You can cuddle sick babies, take shelter dogs on walks, make food boxes for hungry families, or teach single moms how to put a résumé together. Be a mentor to an at-risk youth. I'm telling you, whatever your strengths or interests are, there is an organization that would love to have you volunteer. Your like-minded people are out there. You may have to work a little to find them. Don't let that stop you from seeking out the people who will fill your heart with love, purpose, and joy.

## EXERCISE: MAKE A PERSONAL CONTRACT

Once you are clear about your values, make a contract with yourself for how you are going to live within your value system. At my practice, we have clients write out a Wellness Plan. This document has four components. The first is a list of unhealthy behaviors you once engaged in that don't make sense in your life anymore. Things like "Agreeing to do things I don't want to do, screaming at my spouse, staying up past midnight, working more than forty hours a week," and the like go on this list. These are just examples, and based on your values, you will decide what behaviors are problem behaviors for you.

The second section is comprised of triggers. Triggers are the internal and external factors in your life that put you at risk for engaging in unhealthy behaviors. An external factor would be if your boss asks you to take on another project even though he knows your plate is full. A situation such as this might be a trigger for you to go back to your old behavior of saying yes to things that aren't good for you. An internal factor might be something like feeling lonely. The inner feeling of loneliness could be a trigger for you to down a carton of ice cream and stay in your house all weekend binge-watching *America's Next Top Model*. Some ideas for what to list as triggers might be "my boss asking me to take on a new project, my boyfriend pressuring me for sex, my mom nagging me about when I'm going to get married, feeling lonely, feeling overwhelmed, self-doubt, or fear of rejection."

Once you have identified your unhealthy behaviors and triggers, list your healthy behaviors—this is the third section. Include healthy alternative behaviors for your problem behaviors, like "call a friend, invite someone out for coffee, or go see a movie or live performance if I feel lonely." You'll also want to include healthy maintenance behaviors.

Healthy maintenance behaviors are the specific commitments you make to yourself to ensure you have incorporated health, wellness, positive relationships, and joy into your life. Don't write things in vague terms like "exercise more" or "practice gratitude." I encourage you to be as specific as possible so you have a measure of your self-love practice. "Go to my kickboxing class at least twice per week, write one gratitude every day in my gratitude journal, meditate for ten minutes each morning, take my husband on a date twice a month, and get the kids together for a family game night on Tuesdays" are some examples. Again, this list should reflect your values and how you will be incorporating them on a daily, weekly, and monthly basis.

Finally, the fourth section is to identify some accountability partners. These should be friends or family members whom you trust with the most intimate details of your life. People with whom you feel safe to say, "Hey, I'm working on taking better care of myself, loving myself more, and making healthier choices. I want to tell you what I'm working on and ask you to check in with me and help me stay accountable." These should be people who don't have a personal agenda with you. Let's face it. As much as I love my husband and want what is best for him, I also want him to do what I tell him to do. I'm not really the greatest accountability partner to him because of my vested interest in his behavior.

Ideally, you should have five people in your life who can serve this purpose. Of course, you should offer to do the same for them, opening the door to a meaningful, emotionally intimate relationship in which you are able to mutually share the more vulnerable parts of yourself safely. Look for and be the kind of accountability partner who is willing to offer empathy and support, who is ready to call out BS when you see it, and who will hold someone's feet to the fire from a place of love and good intention.

I don't want my accountability partners to always agree with me or tell me I'm right. My truest friends call me out. They tell me when I'm being too rigid or unkind, or when I'm overreacting. I do the same for them because we love each other and want each of us to be our happiest, healthiest, best selves. Sometimes you need someone who loves you enough to give you a dose of reality to set you straight.

## Check Your Attitude

Finally, I want to talk about the attitude with which you walk through the world. How do you encourage healthy, positive thoughts and intervene on harmful, negative thinking? Your answer will be a primary factor in how successful you are at loving yourself, loving others, living a happy life, and maintaining a peaceful heart.

Recall the saying that states whether you are looking for the good or the bad in a situation, you are sure to find it. The truth is, there is good and bad everywhere. People who focus on the negative in life usually aren't miserable beings just looking for a reason to be unhappy. People who focus on the positive aren't necessarily naïve or in denial. Both sets of people are living in and responding to their realities. They are choosing which parts of their realities they are going to give their attention.

It keeps coming back to that pesky negativity bias, which places emphasis on potential danger. Thank goodness for this cognitive function. It keeps us alive and safe. I am grateful for it. Unfortunately, it also prevents us from giving weight to all the good that happens around us. From an evolutionary perspective, that warm, fuzzy stuff just isn't as important. If we were still living in the wild, trying not to walk through poison ivy or have our babies dragged off by wolves, we might not have time to focus on that glorious sunset or the peaceful quiet of a walk among the trees.

Our brains just haven't caught up with the times. In our modern lives, you can have dozens of positive interactions with your spouse, for example, but as soon as he forgets to pick up milk on the way home, it's so easy to jump into "You always do this! You're so undependable! I have to do everything myself around here." We must make intentional efforts to focus on all the parts of our reality, not just the immediate thoughts and emotions that come surging in when we are upset, anxious, disappointed, or uncertain. When you find yourself talking in extremes, like "I always" or "you never" statements, take a breath. That's your cue to pause, regroup, collect your wisest self, and revisit the situation from a grounded, balanced place.

The dysfunctional ways you respond to life today are probably a result of the same adaptive methods you developed to survive hardships earlier in your life. You might have lived a life in which you really couldn't count on others, where you had to do everything yourself. Your survival instincts were strong. You have every right to appreciate those adaptive parts of you.

It might not be true today that your spouse is undependable or that you must do everything around the house yourself. Those thoughts may be your old survival system kicking into gear and causing a reactive response. What helped you survive long ago may be unhelpful, unwarranted, and even destructive today. It is imperative to maintain self-awareness around how you respond to stressors in your life now. You can and should express gratitude to the survivor parts of you, but if they are interfering with your ability to be your best self today, it's time to throw those parts a retirement party and let them go.

## EXERCISE: GET A REMINDER RING

Changing the way you do life is hard at first. It takes constant practice and reinforcement. I suggest you get a reminder to wear on your hands, like a ring. You'll want something you see many times every day that can remind you of the changes you are making. If your struggle is gratitude, call it your gratitude ring. Every time you notice it throughout the day, remind yourself of one thing for which you are grateful. If you are struggling to use a kind inner voice, call it your affirmation ring. Think of a positive truth about yourself every time you see it. Whether your ring exists to remind you to be less reactive, more compassionate, nonjudgmental, or something else, having a constant reminder is an excellent way to help you change your unhelpful patterns of thinking until it becomes second nature.

I have a single friend who bought what looked like a wedding ring to wear as a reminder of "the committed relationship I am in with myself." I love that sentiment. You can't commit wholly to anything until you've committed wholly to you.

## Takeaways and Talking Points

✦ You are ready to build a joyful life. Start by distinguishing your destructive comfort-seeking behaviors from real self-care.

✦ Clarify your values by making a values list.

✦ Create a personal contract so you have a plan with objective measures for success.

✦ Changing your attitude and your life is hard work. You'll need reminders and reinforcement while you train your brain to think differently. Get a reminder ring. It will help.

# CONCLUSION

*You can't go back and make a new start,*
*but you can start right now and*
*make a brand new ending.*

—James R. Sherman

Congratulations! You've come to the end of this book, which may be just the beginning of your journey on the path to loving yourself and changing your life. I hope you feel excited, empowered, and ready to realize your potential. Your best life is out there, and your best self is already inside you, waiting for permission to take the driver's seat. Let's take a moment to summarize the steps outlined throughout this book to give you a sturdy launching pad for your journey.

**Step One:** Evaluate your internal voice. We all have an internal voice, which is a composite of all the voices we have heard throughout our lives. Often, that voice can be unkind and critical. In this step, examine what kind of statements you make to yourself, about yourself. What are the negative core beliefs you hold about yourself that drive your unhelpful self-talk? Identify whose voice is driving the unkind statements you make to yourself in your head. Actively practice rejecting that voice and make intentional efforts to listen to and strengthen the kind, encouraging voice that is your true, original voice.

***Step Two:*** Unpack your personal trauma history. Create a trauma egg. Get your story out on paper. Now is the time to stop minimizing your painful life experiences and honor the younger versions of yourself whose pain is still real inside you. Those unhealed parts of you drive the inner critic who lives in your head. Your self-defeating voice emerged to protect you from painful experiences, but today it is just the voice of fear. It's time to get that voice out of the driver's seat.

The days of stuffing down and ignoring your pain need to end. Getting your trauma out on paper can be the first step in healing your old emotional wounds. I know it can be scary to think about facing the hurt you have been running from for years. It takes courage to look at the younger versions of yourself and say, "I see you. I see your pain." Although painful, allowing your body and heart to move through the grieving process completely will free you from the suffering you store deep inside.

Many people fear that acknowledging their pain will break them, that they will be trapped in that sadness and won't be able to escape. You need to fight past that fear. You can feel your pain and move through to the other side of it. Acknowledging your hurt will not trap you in it. If you broke your arm, would you ignore the pain, hoping it would just go away if you don't think about it? Of course not. You would listen to your body, acknowledge the reality of your wound, seek medical help, and do what you needed to do, even if it was uncomfortable, so you could heal properly and move on.

Step Two follows this same philosophy for healing your heart. I am compelled now to reiterate that if you have a significant trauma history, this step may require the help of a specialized therapist. Give yourself that gift. You deserve it.

***Step Three:*** Build your self-worth. This step is a little different for everyone based on your personal challenges. We all tell ourselves lies about why we don't deserve happiness. Ask yourself now, "What steps do I need to take to feel worthy of living my best life?" Step Three is about removing your internal barriers to joy and self-approval. Your Step Three may look like forgiving yourself, letting go of shame, making amends, ending toxic relationships, practicing self-compassion, and/ or developing a relationship with yourself and your feelings.

The hallmark of Step Three, irrespective of how you do it, is to begin treating yourself with compassion, care, and respect. You have always deserved to treat yourself this way. Your painful, early life experiences and the self-defeating thoughts that emerged because of them have tricked you into believing you aren't worthy of your own love and care. Engaging in a self-compassion practice will help you find self-acceptance and begin building your internal sense of worthiness.

Step Three often involves asking yourself questions to ensure you are treating yourself with compassion, care, and respect. You may want to ask yourself questions like these:

- ✦ "How would a person who really loves themselves respond to this?"
- ✦ "Is saying yes to this request going to be harmful to me in some way?"
- ✦ "If I believed I was worthy of love and respect, would I tolerate this behavior?"
- ✦ "Would I be willing to behave this way if I loved and respected myself?"

You must believe you are worthy of love and happiness if you hope to create the life you desire. Then you can use your self-worth to muster the bravery required to overcome the fears that get in the way of chasing your dreams.

***Step Four:*** Self-empowerment! Step Four is where the work of interacting differently with the world begins. Now that you feel worthy of compassion, care, and respect, you will begin teaching others how to treat you differently. You will do this by advocating for yourself and your needs while simultaneously considering and honoring others. Remember, an empowered person is not demanding, rude, or rigid. Healthy self-empowerment requires you to master the art of assertiveness, not aggressiveness. You will set healthy boundaries in this step, and though you will probably feel some growing pains as you change your interactions with others, you will also begin feeling the buds of self-love blossoming inside you!

There are many fun exercises you can use to begin feeling more empowered. Positive psychology encourages us to focus on what is going well and build from there. Make an affirmation list, start a gratitude journal, set a daily intention, practice learned optimism, make self-love art, and set realistic but challenging goals. These are all excellent ways to build your self-esteem, create a positive outlook, and prepare yourself for the hard work of self-growth.

***Step Five:*** Self-growth. It's time to give up your unhealthy ways of being. This is the step where you'll have to give yourself some tough love. As important as it is to acknowledge your feelings, honor your unmet needs, and hold others accountable for how they treat you, you need to hold yourself accountable, too. We can't talk about ending toxic relationships without realistically looking at our own toxicity. This includes the toxic ways you treat yourself and the toxic ways you treat others. If you want to live in your light, you must acknowledge your darkness.

We reviewed the most common types of cognitive distortions and tools for reframing these faulty ways of thinking. You mustn't let yourself off the hook in this step. If the only toxic behaviors you can identify about yourself sound like, "I pick people who hurt/abuse/abandon me," or "I attract unhealthy people," or "I'm a caretaker/rescuer," you haven't looked deep enough. These statements are akin to a humble-brag. They present you as a martyr and don't make you take ownership of what is really going on with you at your most unhealthy level.

I want you to look at the ways you are defensive, offensive, passive-aggressive, stubborn, selfish, manipulative, and victim-posturing. Only when you are willing to face the underbelly of your own dysfunction can you shift the way you think and behave in meaningful ways. People who love themselves fully do not live in denial about their ugliness. They acknowledge it and work actively to change it. Create a cost-benefit analysis, and explore the payoff for staying just as you are today. Then examine the benefits of changing your behavior. You will need to consider all that you will lose and gain if you choose to continue down this path toward love and emotional health. Your mission, should you choose to accept it, will lead you to Step Six, where you'll create a new way of living.

**Step Six:** Master a healthy way of being. In this step, you will replace your unhealthy behaviors with healthier, more adaptive ones. We began this lesson by exploring the concept of inner peace. You will develop this practice by using skills such as radical acceptance, self-compassion, mindfulness, and self-acceptance. Practicing non-judgment of self and others is an essential component of this step. Another chief principal of Step Six is accepting what you can and cannot control and learning to let go in situations of the latter. Finally, you will build failure into your game plan for self-growth so it doesn't knock you off course when it inevitably happens. Through cultivating a self-care practice that is grounded in your new sense of self-worth, you'll build resiliency as you forge ahead.

***Step Seven:*** Foster a life of joy and purpose. This is the fun part! In this step you define your values and create a life built around those values. This step is the reward for all the hard work you have put in thus far. Here you get to reap the benefits of your self-growing pains and incorporate healthy relationships, play, laughter, real self-care, adventure, and meaning into your life. You will also make a personal contract to hold yourself accountable. Next comes the good stuff. Chase your wildest, craziest dream, or live as simply and gently as your heart desires. You are the master of your destiny and the author of the rest of your life's story. Make it a good one.

✦ ✦ ✦

So there you have it. A road map for the path to overcoming your past, becoming your best, healthiest self, and living the life of your dreams. These seven steps are simple enough in theory, but mastering them could be your greatest challenge. I may not know you, but I believe in you. I believe in your goodness, your worth, your strength, and your capability. I believe in you because you are a survivor. You have come this far, and you have a hunger to be better than you are today. You long for a different kind of life. That hunger, that longing, your survival thus far, all tell me you are a fighter. You are fighting for yourself right now, and it's beautiful. Messy, perhaps, but beautiful.

All journeys eventually meet their end, and we have reached the point where you are ready to continue traveling the path of self-love without me. Though we part ways here, I pray you keep my words of hope and resiliency in your heart as you continue onward. I honor you now as you set out to stop just surviving and begin thriving in a life as beautiful as you can imagine. May your spirit be ever hungry and your heart forever full. Safe travels, gentle warrior.

# REFERENCES AND RECOMMENDED READING

Beck, Aaron. *Cognitive Therapy and the Emotional Disorders.* New York, NY: Penguin, 1979.

Brown, Brené. *Daring Greatly.* New York, NY: Avery, 2015.

Felitti, Vincent J., Robert F. Anda, Dale Nordenberg, David F. Williamson, Alison M. Spitz, Valerie Edwards, Mary P. Koss, James S. Marks. "Relationship of Childhood Abuse and Household Dysfunction to Many of the Leading Causes of Death in Adults." *American Journal of Preventive Medicine* 14 (1998): 245–258. https://doi.org/10.1016/S0749-3797(98)00017-8.

Grandin, Temple. *Animals Make Us Human.* New York, NY: Mariner Books, 2010.

Hay, Louise. *You Can Heal Your Life.* Carlsbad, CA: Hay House, 1984.

Linehan, Marsha. *DBT Skills Training Manual.* New York, NY: The Guilford Press, 2014.

Murray, Marilyn. *The Murray Method.* Scottsdale, AZ: Vivo Publications, 2012.

Neff, Kristin. *Self-Compassion: The Proven Power of Being Kind to Yourself.* New York, NY: William Morrow Paperbacks, 2015.

Seligman, Martin. *Learned Optimism.* New York, NY: Vintage, 2006.

Stevens, Jane Ellen. "Addiction Doc Says: It's Not the Drugs. It's the ACEs… Adverse Childhood Experiences." *ACES Too High News* (2017). Accessed April 1, 2018. https://acestoohigh.com/2017/05/02/addiction-doc-says-stop-chasing-the-drug-focus-on-aces-people-can-recover/.

# APPENDIX

## Adverse Childhood Experience (ACE) Questionnaire

### *Finding Your ACE Score*

While you were growing up, during your first eighteen years of life,

1. Did a parent or other adult in the household often . . .

   Swear at you, insult you, put you down, or humiliate you?

   *or*

   Act in a way that made you afraid that you might be physically hurt?

   ❑ Yes ❑ No *If yes, enter 1:* _____

2. Did a parent or other adult in the household often . . .

   Push, grab, slap, or throw something at you?

   *or*

   Ever hit you so hard that you had marks or were injured?

   ❑ Yes ❑ No *If yes, enter 1:* _____

3. Did an adult or person at least five years older than you ever . . .

   Touch or fondle you or have you touch their body in a sexual way?

   *or*

   Try to or actually have oral, anal, or vaginal sex with you?

   ❑ Yes ❑ No *If yes, enter 1:* _____

4. Did you often feel that . . .

No one in your family loved you or thought you were important or special?

*or*

Your family didn't look out for each other, feel close to each other, or support each other?

❑ Yes  ❑ No  *If yes, enter 1:* _____

5. Did you often feel that . . .

You didn't have enough to eat, had to wear dirty clothes, and had no one to protect you?

*or*

Your parents were too drunk or high to take care of you or take you to the doctor if you needed it?

❑ Yes  ❑ No  *If yes, enter 1:* _____

6. Were your parents ever separated or divorced?

❑ Yes  ❑ No  *If yes, enter 1:* _____

7. Was your mother or stepmother:

Often pushed, grabbed, slapped, or had something thrown at her?

*or*

Sometimes or often kicked, bitten, hit with a fist, or hit with something hard?

*or*

Ever repeatedly hit over at least a few minutes or threatened with a gun or knife?

❑ Yes  ❑ No  *If yes, enter 1:* _____

8. Did you live with anyone who was a problem drinker or alcoholic or who used street drugs?

❑ Yes  ❑ No  *If yes, enter 1:* _____

9. Was a household member depressed or mentally ill, or did a household member attempt suicide?

❑ Yes ❑ No *If yes, enter 1:* _____

10. Did a household member go to prison?

❑ Yes ❑ No *If yes, enter 1:* _____

Now add up your "Yes" answers: _____ This is your ACE Score.

# ABOUT THE AUTHOR

**D**r. Heidi Green is a licensed clinical psychologist at Psychological Counseling Services, a world-renowned center for trauma and addiction treatment in Scottsdale, Arizona. Her interest in trauma healing stems from her own story of childhood trauma and recovery. Over the years, her training and experience illuminated the significance of early childhood experiences in the development of self-worth. Similarities in patient stories revealed that regardless of time passed, unresolved childhood wounds continue to plague adults in the form of low self-esteem, self-criticism, and unhealthy coping mechanisms. This realization set her on a quest to formulate a path to self-love and ultimately served as the inspiration for this book.

In addition to her therapy practice, Dr. Green facilitates in-person workshops focused on trauma healing, self-compassion, and self-love. She maintains an active social media presence on Instagram at the handle @drheidigreen, where she provides education and inspiration on a range of mental health topics. She regularly answers mental health questions posed by her followers and creates informational videos on her IGTV channel. Dr. Green also creates online workshops focusing on emotional health and healing which can be found on her website, *drheidigreen.com.*